GOD'S WRATH On *Left Behind*

Exposing the Antichrist Agenda
of the *Left Behind* Series

GOD'S WRATH On *Left Behind*

Exposing the Antichrist Agenda of the *Left Behind* Series

Lisa Ruby

GOD'S WRATH On *Left Behind*

Exposing the Antichrist Agenda of the *Left Behind* Series

Copyright ©2002 by Lisa Ruby
Liberty To The Captives Publications
www.libertytothecaptives.net

All rights reserved. No part of this book may be reproduced or transmitted in any form or by any means, electronic or mechanical, including photocopying, recording, or by any information storage and retrieval system, without written permission from the author, except for the inclusion of brief quotations in a review.

All scripture references are from the King James Bible.

Left Behind is a registered trademark of Tyndale House Publishers, Inc.

Printed in the United States of America.

International Standard Book Number: 0-9721264-0-6

Book cover design by Alpha Advertising
http://www.alphaadvertising.com/covers/

LEFT BEHIND:
FINISHING OFF THE FALLING AWAY

Satan is already working in the world and the church, but once He who is preventing him from having full reign steps out of his way, the tribulation will begin.

> For the mystery of iniquity doth already work: only he who now letteth will let, until he be taken out of the way. (2 Thess. 2:7)

The Holy Spirit will not stop restraining the full expression of Satan's iniquity until the falling away, or apostasy, of the church occurs.

> Let no man deceive you by any means: for that day shall not come, except there come a falling away first, and that man of sin be revealed, the son of perdition. (2 Thess. 2:3)

The order of this is set in scripture and cannot be broken – first the falling away, then the tribulation – but *when* this actually occurs has much to do with the people of God. If the church continues her descent away from the holy faith of Jesus, she will have reached the point of having fallen completely away from her First Love. When this occurs, Satan will take his place "as God" in the church. This is the Falling Away. When this happens, God will treat the earth the way He did in the days of Noah, but instead of a flood, he will allow Satan to have his time of open worldwide worship and rule.

The endtimes apostasy has already begun, and the *Left Behind* series is finishing the job. *God's Wrath on Left Behind* is God's *real* second chance for the church to repent and return to her First Love. Satan is sitting in the *Left Behind* series as if he were God. Will you continue to believe his lies?

TABLE OF CONTENTS

1	*LEFT BEHIND:* FINISHING OFF THE FALLING AWAY	v
1	THE ANTI-CHRISTIAN GOSPEL OF *LEFT BEHIND*	1
2	ENTERTAINMENT: THE BEST TOOL FOR PROPAGANDA	13
3	A CERTAIN MANNER OF AN AFFAIR IS NOTHING TO FEEL GUILTY ABOUT?	17
4	*NICOLAE* AND PRO-ABORTION PROPAGANDA	29
5	CHILD MURDER AND SUICIDE: OPTIONS FOR CHRISTIANS DURING THE TRIBULATION?	49
6	DISAPPEARANCES: THE BEST-KEPT SECRET	61
7	THE BIBLE ON THE MARK OF THE BEAST	83
8	BY THEIR MARKS YE SHALL KNOW THEM?	95
9	SATAN ON THE MARK OF THE BEAST	111
10	SEX AND THE *LEFT BEHIND* SERIES	133
11	THE ANTICHRIST FOUNDATION OF THE *LEFT BEHIND* SERIES	143
12	MERGING WITH THE KINGDOM OF ANTICHRIST	163
13	NEW AGE MARKINGS ON *LEFT BEHIND*	175
14	SATAN'S SOUL HARVEST	187

ESSENTIAL APPENDICES

THE GOSPEL OF JESUS CHRIST	197
WHAT DOES IT MEAN TO BE A TRUE CHRISTIAN	201
NOTES	211

And if any man shall take away from the words of the book of this prophecy, God shall take away his part out of the book of life, and out of the holy city, and from the things which are written in this book.

He which testifieth these things saith, Surely I come quickly. Amen. Even so, come, Lord Jesus.

The grace of our Lord Jesus Christ be with you all. Amen.

Revelation 22:19-21

1

THE ANTI-CHRISTIAN GOSPEL OF *LEFT BEHIND*

The gospel is the history of the birth, life, actions, death, resurrection, ascension and doctrines of Jesus Christ; it is a revelation of the grace of God to fallen man through a mediator, including the character, actions, and doctrines of Christ, with the whole scheme of salvation, as revealed by Christ and His apostles. This gospel is said to have been preached to Abraham, by the promise "in thee shall all nations be blessed" (Gal. 3:8).[1]

The gospel is the revelation of Jesus Christ, and His narrow way, that leads to life. The *Left Behind* series is a promotion of Satan's broad road that leads to destruction in the guise of "tribulation-style" Christianity.

The Phony Grace of the *Left Behind* Series

The *Left Behind* series presents a *false* grace through "Christian" characters that give in to ungodliness and worldly lusts that war against their souls. The storyline has the characters sinning to survive and rationalizing their service to sin because they are living during the tribulation. The grace that brings genuine salvation teaches every person who possesses it the same thing, even during the tribulation:

> For the grace of God that bringeth salvation hath appeared to all men,
> Teaching us that, denying ungodliness and worldly lusts, we should live soberly, righteously, and godly, in this present world;
> Looking for that blessed hope, and the glorious appearing of the great God and our Saviour Jesus Christ;
> Who gave himself for us, that he might redeem us from all iniquity, and purify unto himself a peculiar people, zealous of good works. (Titus 2:11-14)

Jesus Christ gave Himself not only to rescue us from hell, but also to redeem us from *all* iniquity and to purify unto Himself a peculiar people. Those saved by grace are peculiar people, purified unto Jesus and set apart singly *unto* Him.

The Bible says that we are saved by grace through faith, and not of works, lest any man should boast (see Eph. 2:8-9).

> And if by grace, then is it no more of works: otherwise grace is no more grace. But if it be of works, then it is no more grace: otherwise work is no more work. (Rom. 11:6)

We cannot work to acquire salvation, because the only atonement for sin is the sinless blood of Jesus. When we are saved by grace, we become God's workmanship, created in Christ Jesus unto good works which God has already ordained that we should *walk* in them (see Eph. 2:10). When we are saved by the true grace of God we are: created unto good works (Eph. 2:10), zealous of good works (Titus 2:14), full of good works (Acts 9:36), rich in good works (1 Tim. 6:18), thoroughly furnished unto good works (2 Tim. 3:17), show a pattern of good works (Titus 2:7), and are careful to maintain good works (Titus 3:8).

> "In the spiritual realm, it is all about Lordship. Who is Lord over your life? Who sits on the throne of your life and has ultimate control of your life? If your answer to those questions is "I am," then you are a spiritual rebel and not under the authority or Lordship of Christ and therefore not a part of His Kingdom. Jesus is Lord in His Kingdom and we are His servants, which mean we surrender control and final say of our lives to Him to become His workmanship."[2]

The works of the members of the Tribulation Force are works of darkness. Their works are not a manifestation of the truth in Jesus Christ, but a manifestation of Satan's values of denying Jesus and serving self. Examples of their sinful lives are provided throughout this book.

Christians Are Not *Still* Sinners Saved by Grace

Forgiveness of sin cannot be obtained by good works, but good works are definitely the result and an out flowing of true salvation.

The false gospel of the *Left Behind* series perverts this truth and gives the reader the idea that Christians are still sinners saved by grace:

> "They kept encouraging me to go to this women's Bible study, so finally I went. I was just sure it was going to be more of the same – frumpy middle-aged women talking about being sinners saved by grace." (*Tribulation Force*, p. 409)

Here is yet another example where the authors teach that Christians are just sinners saved by grace:

> "It doesn't make any difference, Hattie. Even people who were raptured with Christ were just sinners saved by grace." (*Soul Harvest*, p. 390)

The doctrine that Christians are "sinners saved by grace" is Satan's invention so that Christians will identify themselves with him instead of with Jesus Christ. The Bible says the saved are the righteous and the lost are sinners. In fact, sinners are the opposite of the righteous in the Scriptures. Those who have not turned from their sins and surrendered to the authority of Jesus Christ are sinners. Those who *have* turned from their sins and submitted to the authority of the Lord Jesus Christ, are the righteous.

Instead of being sinners saved by grace, Christians are *ex-sinners saved by grace*. They crucify the sinful desires of the flesh daily because they know the life they live in the flesh is lived by the faith of the Son of God, who loved them and gave Himself for them (see Gal. 2:20).

Jesus said,

> "They that are whole have no need of the physician, but they that are sick: I came not to call the righteous, but sinners to repentance." (Mark 2:17)

Jesus came to call sinners. Once the sinner is turned from darkness to light and from the power of Satan unto God, he becomes "the righteous." The righteous have ceased to serve self and sin, and instead, sincerely love the Lord Jesus Christ. The sinner loves sin and self and hates the *real* Lord Jesus Christ.

Yes, a righteous person has the ability to sin, but with his mind he serves the law of God (Rom. 7:25). He wants to serve God, and is grieved when he sins. He is not a sinner, even though he does sin at times. Sinfulness does not characterize him. He is righteous. Righteousness characterizes him. The righteous reckons himself dead to sin and lives unto righteousness (see 1 Pet. 2:24). When he sins he confesses and forsakes it immediately. He presses on toward the mark of the high calling of God in Christ Jesus. He wants to be perfect like Jesus, and has a mind to be so. He is sensitive to the Holy Spirit and is always ready to repent when God reveals that he is being otherwise-minded (see Phil. 3:14-15).

This is not so with the sinner. With his mind he serves the law of sin. He neither confesses nor forsakes sin. He loves to be his own authority. The Bible says he is dead in his trespasses and sins and will stay that way until he is quickened or given life by faith in the Lord Jesus Christ (see Eph. 2:1).

For the sinner, sinning is the rule. For the righteous, sinning is the *exception* to the rule. Sinners walk according to the course of this world. The righteous, in manifesting the truth, overcome the world (see Eph. 2:2, 1 John 5:4).

The sinner and the righteous are two opposite kinds of people:

> Therefore the ungodly shall not stand in the judgment, nor sinners in the congregation of the righteous. (Ps. 1:5)

> And if the righteous scarcely be saved, where shall the ungodly and the sinner appear? (1 Pet. 4:18)

Christians *were* sinners saved by grace. They are *now* saints, who present their bodies daily as living sacrifices, holy and acceptable unto the Lord, which is their reasonable sacrifice (see Rom. 12:1).

God Shows Grace While We Continue in Sin?

Bruce Barnes explained to Rayford and Chloe why he was "left behind" and did not disappear in the "rapture." He was not a sincere Christian, but was a phony who pretended to be devout.

The authors inserted a print subliminal through Bruce's explanation about not living right as a Christian:

> "I just kept getting forgiveness because I thought God was bound to do that." (*Left Behind*, p. 195)

Bruce should have been made to say he *thought* he kept getting forgiveness, but he was wrong. By having Bruce say he kept getting forgiveness, the authors communicated that we are under grace while we continue in sin. The Bible says a Christian's forgiveness for sins is not automatic, but is conditioned upon his "walking in the light":

> But if we walk in the light, as he is in the light, we have fellowship one with another, and the blood of Jesus Christ his Son cleanseth us from all sin. (1 John 1:7)

Bruce went on to say that he knew the Bible said one had to "believe and receive, to "trust and abide," but he did not really understand what it meant:

> "I wanted the bottom line, the easiest route, the simplest path. I knew other verses said that we are not to continue in sin just because God shows grace." (*Left Behind*, p. 195)

The false message in Bruce's statement is that God shows grace when we continue in sin. We are not to take advantage of God just because he shows grace as we continue in sin. This is an antichrist message about grace. The Bible teaches that grace reigns through righteousness, not while we continue in sin:

> That as sin hath reigned unto death, even so might grace reign through righteousness unto eternal life through Jesus Christ our Lord. (Rom. 5:21)

> What shall we say then? Shall we continue in sin, that grace may abound? God forbid. (Rom. 6:1)

Paul did not reassure Christians that grace will abound while they continue in sin. He even repeated this precept later in his letter:

> There is therefore now no condemnation to them which are in Christ Jesus, who walk not after the flesh, but after the Spirit. (Rom. 8:1)

Grace reigns through righteousness, no condemnation is to them that walk after the Spirit, and cleansing of sins is for those who walk in the light. Does this mean that a Christian works *for* his salvation? No, he cannot work for his salvation. Salvation is a gift that the Lord Jesus Christ purchased with His own blood. No person can ever earn or deserve his salvation. However, the person who understands that he does not deserve to be saved must believe the Word of the God which he says he believes in, and work *out* his salvation with fear and trembling:

> Wherefore, my beloved, as ye have always obeyed, not as in my presence only, but now much more in my absence, work out your own salvation with fear and trembling. (Phil. 2:12)

God Will Save You if Your Motive Is Selfish?

Buck reassured Chaim that he could be saved for selfish reasons:

> "But Cameron, can God accept me if my motive is selfish?"
> "We all come to faith selfish in some ways, Chaim. How could it be otherwise? We want to be forgiven. We want to be accepted, received, included. We want to go to heaven instead of hell. We want to be able to face death knowing what comes next." (*The Indwelling*, p. 227)

This is the gospel of the *Left Behind* series in a nutshell. You can be saved for self, live for self, and die with self first and foremost in your heart and mind. This is the gospel of Satan, and that is why he is the god of this world which seeks its own way. Satan's gospel says you can use Jesus to wash away your sins but you do not have to obey Him. Satan says you can hold the free gift of salvation in rebellion to Jesus Christ.

The real gospel of Jesus Christ is about sincerely loving and dying daily for the Lord Jesus Christ who first loved us:

> And he said to *them* all, If any *man* will come after me, let him deny himself, and take up his cross daily, and follow me. (Luke 9:23)

Today there is much evidence of a selfish religion. People want to go to heaven; they claim salvation and justification. There is preaching about justification, but it is isolated from sanctification. Sanctification cannot be separated from justification, i.e., we cannot claim we have received a pardon for our sin if we still love and serve sin.[3]

Salvation is not about selfishness; it is a turning from the self you have served all your life to serve the one who gave Himself for you.

Coming to Christ For Fire Insurance?

> Buck nodded. He understood, but did he know the answer to Chaim's question? People through the ages had all kinds of motives for becoming believers, and surely fear was a common one. He'd heard Bruce Barnes say that people sometimes come to Christ for fire insurance – to stay out of hell – only to later realize all the benefits that come with that policy. (*The Indwelling*, p. 228-29)

The following is an accurate description of "fire insurance Christianity": "Most today want to claim Jesus as Savior, but not as Lord over their lives. I have been told, 'Well, I've made Jesus my Savior, but I haven't made Him Lord of my life yet.' Wrong! If He is not Lord, He is not savior."[3]

> For if after they have escaped the pollutions of the world through the knowledge of the Lord and Saviour Jesus Christ, they are again entangled therein, and overcome, the latter end is worse with them than the beginning. (2 Pet. 2:20)

Bruce said that some come to Christ for this reason "only to later realize all the benefits that come with that policy." Bruce conceded that the fire insurance policy is real but the bearer of it will find out about more benefits later. This kind of phony salvation slays souls. "Fire insurance Christians" are the kind that sow to the flesh and think they will still inherit eternal life. The Bible says they will reap corruption:

> For he that soweth to his flesh shall of the flesh reap corruption; but he that soweth to the Spirit shall of the Spirit reap life everlasting. (Gal. 6:8)

"Fire insurance Christians" think that walking after the flesh will bring them no condemnation. The Bible teaches the opposite:

> There is therefore now no condemnation to them which are in Christ Jesus, who walk not after the flesh, but after the Spirit. (Rom. 8:1)

There is no such thing as "fire insurance Christianity." This antichrist teaching turns the grace of God into lasciviousness, and it denies the only Lord God. It is ungodly men that have been already ordained to condemnation who teach such things (see Jude 1:4).

Nothing Churchy, or Distinctively Christian Either

Bruce Barnes led the first church service after the "disappearances." He did not want the service to be "churchy."

> At two o'clock, when everyone was hungry and tired, Bruce said, "I'm going to have to bring this to a close. One thing I wasn't going to do today was anything traditionally churchy; including singing. But I feel we need to praise the Lord for what has happened here today. Let me teach you a simple chorus of adoration. (*Left Behind*, p. 220)

The "not wanting to be churchy" theme continued throughout the *Left Behind* series. It can also be called the "not wanting to be distinctively Christian" theme. There is no mention of Bruce baptizing anyone – not even Rayford, Buck, or Chloe. Not once do we read of them assembling together to take the Lord's Supper either.

These two distinctively Christian ordinances have been entirely left out of the *Left Behind* series. Baptism is the "answer of a good conscience toward God" (see 1 Pet. 3:21). "Baptism is the seal of an inward spiritual condition that by faith has occurred within the heart of a believer."[4]

> Therefore we are buried with him by baptism into death: that like Christ was raised up from the dead by the glory of the Father, even so we also should walk in newness of life. (Rom. 6:4)

"Water baptism is expected of every believer (Matt. 28: 19, Acts 10:47) and should take place immediately after conversion (Acts 8:12, 13, 36; 10:47; 19:2-6)."[5]

Taking the Lord's Supper shows the Lord's death until He comes. When Christians break the bread and eat it, they do this in remembrance of Jesus' body being broken for them. Jesus *commanded* His followers to remember His body. When Christians take of the cup, they remember the new testament (the new covenant) in His blood. This is Jesus' *command* to His people.

> For as often as ye eat this bread, and drink this cup, ye do shew the Lord's death till he come. (1 Cor. 11:26)

After the church's building was destroyed in the earthquake, there was no more mention of any regular worship services by members of the Tribulation Force. The Bible says that Christians are to do this so much the more as they see the day of the Lord approaching (see Heb. 10:25).

Prayer with fasting was also strangely absent from the storyline. This spiritual discipline is essential to the Christian life, and all the more so during the tribulation when we must draw near to God so he will draw near to us.

Can You Be a True Christian Without Being Willing to Die for the Testimony of Jesus?

Can we be true Christians without being willing to lay down our lives for the testimony of Jesus? The *Left Behind* series teaches that we can and there are many examples of this in the lives of the *Left Behind* characters' "denying Jesus Christ" brand of Christianity.

The message that we can be truly saved but not be willing to give our life for the sake of the testimony of Jesus was presented in a subliminal fashion in a passage in *Nicolae*.

Rayford officiated at Bruce Barnes' funeral service. At the end of the service, after explaining that many will be martyred during the tribulation, he asked a question to the large gathering of people present:

> "I must ask you today, are you prepared? Are you willing? Would you give your life for the sake of the gospel?"
> Rayford paused to take a breath and was started when someone cried out, "I will!"
> Rayford didn't know what to say. Suddenly, from another part of the sanctuary: "So will I!"
> Three or four others said the same in unison. Rayford choked back tears. It had been a rhetorical question. He had not expected an answer. (*Nicolae*, p. 325)

This would be a perfect spot for the authors to have Tsion speak up (he spoke up at another point in the service, even though he was a fugitive and in hiding) and declare that they cannot even be true Christians without having settled this question. But instead, they had Rayford say this was a rhetorical question:

> He continued, his voice thick, "Thank you, brothers and sisters. I fear we may all be called upon to express our willingness to die for the cause. Praise God you are willing. (*Nicolae*, p. 325)

Rayford did not say that unless they are willing to die for the Lord Jesus Christ, then they cannot be His true disciple In fact, the authors gave many examples in the series where Christians did not express willingness to die for Christ and actually denied knowing Him in order to save their own lives in this world.

> The Lord Jesus Christ is the definer of the gospel message, not modern theologians. The issue of what it means to believe must rest with how the Lord defines commitment to himself.[6]

This is precisely the point. Who defines what it is to believe? Is it the Lord Jesus Christ, or the examples of apostate Christianity depicted in the *Left Behind* series where the characters "creatively" deny Jesus Christ before men while the reader is led to believe this is necessary in order to survive during the tribulation?

What Did Jesus Say About Commitment?

Jesus defined commitment to Himself, and it is completely opposite of the bogus Christianity depicted in the *Left Behind* series. Jesus said:

> "If any man come to me, and hate not his father, and mother, and wife, and children, and brethren, and sister, yea, and his own life also, he cannot be my disciple." (Luke 14:26)

The examples of the Christian characters go directly against the words of the Lord Jesus Christ. The authors depicted characters putting their own lives and the lives of family members before their commitment to Jesus Christ. This is why the gospel of the *Left Behind* series is anti-Christian. It is opposed to the pre-eminence of Jesus Christ.

In true Christianity, Jesus comes first, even before our own life:

> If anyone wishes to be a true follower of Christ and share in His kingdom, he must love Jesus Christ more than any other person or thing in this world, and even more than life itself. Any commitment that falls short of this disqualifies a person from being a follower of Christ.[7]

The *Left Behind* series is disqualified from being a true depiction of Christianity in the last days because the characters do not put the interests of the Lord Jesus Christ before their own.

They do, however, look to the interests of another "Christ," and he is not Jesus Christ.

2

ENTERTAINMENT: THE BEST TOOL FOR PROPAGANDA

Fiction can be written and used in a powerfully manipulative way. By the use of certain mind-manipulating writing techniques and trigger words, fiction can be a powerful vehicle to reach the subconscious mind of the reader.

Many of the passages in *Left Behind* and subsequent books are actually working as print subliminals. Subliminal means "existing or functioning below the level of the threshold of consciousness." *Print* subliminals are sentences constructed in such a way that they send messages to the reader's mind without his being aware of what has occurred. They work on the person's mind in a manipulative fashion because the message has bypassed his conscious mind:

> Persuasive messages can be placed into the subconscious without channeling them through the conscious if one knows the proper technique. Studies as early as 1917 suggest that sublimininals work like post hypnotic suggestion. They stay in the subconscious mind until cued.[1]

If the reader does not notice a message presented in print, he will accept it uncritically into his mind *without passing judgment* on it. This is how print can work as a subliminal, just like subliminals on audio tape, television, and movies.

Here is an example of a print subliminal in the *Left Behind* series. Remember, this sentence has been constructed in such a way as to slip a message into the reader's subconscious mind without his being consciously aware of it:

> "We can pray for her, but I'm going to feel pretty useless if I can't do something concrete to get her out of there." (*Tribulation Force,* p. 76)

In this print subliminal, the message is that prayer is not concrete. Concrete, in this context means, "substantially real, or actual." The authors did not have Buck say, "Prayer is not concrete." This would have been too obvious and the reader would have noticed it and rejected this message as being wrong. But first mentioning prayer, and then *contrasting* it with doing something concrete sends the message that prayer is not concrete without his knowing this has happened.

Here is another one:

> We're the guys who follow Ben-Judah and believe in Jesus.
> (*Assassins*, p. 239)

Believing in Jesus *is* to follow Jesus. Why do the authors want the reader to follow a man? Jesus said:

> If any man serve me, let him follow me; and where I am, there shall also my servant be: if any man serve me, him will *my* Father honour. (John 12:26)

Propaganda Techniques

Many propaganda techniques are used in the *Left Behind* series. A few examples of the propaganda techniques used are:

> Appeal to Authority. Cites prominent figures to support a position idea, argument, or course of action.[2]

Bruce Barnes and Tsion Ben-Judah, "the world's most astute Bible scholar," were characters used to introduce courses of action and doctrines against the teachings of scripture. The fact that they are authority figures gives more weight to what they say in the mind of the reader.

> Rationalization. Individuals or groups may use favorable generalities to rationalize questionable acts or beliefs. Vague and pleasant phrases are often used to justify such actions or beliefs.[3]

This propaganda technique was used constantly to justify sinful actions on the characters to the reader, especially the times when they lost the testimony of Jesus and denied Jesus Christ.

> Least of Evils. This is a technique of acknowledging that the course of action being taken is perhaps undesirable but that any alternative would result in an outcome far worse.[4]

This technique was used in an attempt to justify yoking with Antichrist in his employ:

> "Without someone on the inside, Carpathia is going to deceive everyone." (*Tribulation Force,* p. 238)

Still other techniques were used in the *Left Behind* series:

> Card stacking or selective omission. This is the process of choosing from a variety of facts only those which support the propagandist's purpose. In using this technique, facts are selected and presented which most effectively strengthen and authenticate the point of view of the propagandist.[5]

This technique was used in the "disappearances" theme. Only the facts which supported the idea that disappearances meant the rapture occurred were given credence in the storyline. Other conclusions were addressed, but discounted to aid in the cardstacking.

> Repetition: an idea or position is repeated in an attempt to elicit an almost automatic response from the audience or to reinforce an audience's opinion or attitude [6]

This technique was used throughout the series to reinforce concepts the authors wanted to sink into the reader's mind. Here are a few examples of concepts the authors repeated many times throughout the series:

1. The "mark of the believer" doctrine.
2. The "disappearances means that the rapture has taken place" doctrine.

3. The "tribulation means that God is trying to get your attention" doctrine.

There are many more propaganda techniques utilized in the *Left Behind* series. "Skillfully used propaganda can take a person from an apparently fixed and immovable position and lead him where he does not want to go without his being aware of it, over paths that he will not notice."[7]

3

A CERTAIN MANNER OF AN AFFAIR IS NOTHING TO FEEL GUILTY ABOUT?

The opening sentence of *Left Behind* is certainly an eye-catcher:

> Rayford Steele's mind was on a woman he had never touched.
> (*Left Behind*, p. 1)

The first sentence in *Left Behind* directs the reader's mind to the topic of adultery, although the biblical term is passed up for the softer-sounding word "affair." Using this topic in a work of fiction asserted to be "hung upon a biblical outline" is not a problem as long as adultery, whether physical or mental, is consistently dealt with according to biblical principles.

We only need to turn to page two to see some serious problems with the way adultery is being handled in the story. Even more troubling is that this trend continues throughout the entire book.

Adultery Takes Moves, Patter, and Style?

During the time Rayford's marriage to Irene was the rockiest, he avoided being home as much as possible.

> Irene accused him of all manner of affairs, and because she was wrong, he denied them with great vigor and, he felt, justified anger.
> (*Left Behind*, p. 144)

It is important to note that Rayford's secret mental and emotional alliance later on with Hattie was definitely a manner of an affair, even though it had not yet degenerated to the point of a physically intimate relationship. Repeatedly throughout the book, the authors promoted the false idea that Rayford and Hattie not only did not have any manner of an affair, but they did not even have a relationship.

> The truth was, he was hoping for and angling for just what she was charging. What frustrated him so was that, despite his looks and bearing, it just wasn't in him to pull it off. He didn't have the moves, the patter, the style. (*Left Behind*, p. 144)

The writers took the sin of adultery and used positive words to describe the person who ensnares others into partaking with him in it! "Moves, patter, and style" sounds far better than "furtiveness, deceitfulness, and sleaze," does it not? Satan is an expert at making sin appealing, and we need to constantly guard our hearts by rejecting the lie that adultery is connected with class, and remember that he who pursues this sin (whether he actually physically commits it or not) destroys his own soul.

Rayford Was Not Unfaithful to Irene?

> Had Irene known how hard he was trying to be unfaithful, she would have left him. (*Left Behind*, p. 144)

The idea presented here is that Rayford was not unfaithful to Irene. He most definitely *was* unfaithful, even though his disloyalty did not culminate in sexual infidelity.

The next sentence is an example of unfaithfulness, although the writers used the preceding sentence to "set up" the reader into thinking this kind of behavior is not unfaithful.

> As it was, he had indulged in that make-out session at the Christmas party before Raymie was born, but he was so inebriated he could hardly remember it. (*Left Behind*, p. 144)

Rayford "made out" with a woman who was not his wife, but the narrative indicated he had never been unfaithful to Irene. Unfaithfulness, or disloyalty, begins in the heart and mind, long before any physical acts of sexual adultery occur.

A Single Woman Touching and Flirting With a Married Man is Not Inappropriate?

I doubt that any wife would agree that Hattie's actions towards Rayford were not inappropriate. A single woman resting her hand on the shoulder of a married man is definitely engaging in inappropriate behavior.

Let us look at some examples in *Left Behind* where a single woman touching and flirting with a married man is depicted as not being wrong. The following sentence reveals Rayford's thoughts about Hattie, the single flight attendant with whom he was having a mental adulterous relationship:

> What he enjoyed most was that she was a toucher. Nothing inappropriate, nothing showy. She simply touched his arm as she brushed past or rested her hand gently on his shoulder when she stood behind his seat in the cockpit. (*Left Behind*, p. 2)

After His Wife Disappeared, Rayford Was Ashamed of the Way He Chased After Hattie Durham

> How ashamed he was of that silly pursuit! For all he knew, Hattie was innocent. She had never bad-mouthed his wife or the fact that he was married. She had never suggested anything inappropriate, at least not for her age. Young people were more touchy and flirtatious, and she claimed no moral or religious code. (*Left Behind*, p. 145)

There is some interesting manipulation here. First, the writers had Rayford justify Hattie's behavior: "She might have been innocent, for all he knew." The authors presented the idea that Hattie might have been innocent of any wrongdoing, even though she deliberately touched him when she had the opportunity, and had dinner alone with him, knowing all the while that he was married.

Then they had him think that she had never suggested anything inappropriate *for her age*. This gives the impression that since young people are more "touchy and flirtatious," it is normal for them to behave like this towards other people, married or not. The more biblically accurate words for such behavior are "strange woman" and "forward."

The reader is being conditioned and desensitized into thinking that affectionate physical contact and flirting between a married man and a younger, single woman is perfectly harmless and not at all inappropriate as long as neither one purposes to turn the relationship onto a sexual path. Neither person would need to plan this because the physical act of adultery would eventually occur under such conditions.

Rayford Had No Reason to Feel Guilty?

Rayford was wondering why he felt guilty:

> Where was this guilt coming from? He had locked eyes with Hattie numerous times, and they had spent hours alone together over dinners in various cities. (*Left Behind*, p. 145)

This is subtly presented as *not* being the basis for feeling guilty because the next sentence explains the things that did *not* happen:

> But she had never asked him to her room or tried to kiss him or even hold his hand. (*Left Behind*, pp. 145-46)

"Locking eyes with Hattie and spending hours alone together over dinners in various cities" is not something to feel guilty about because it had not gone any farther? This message is terribly dangerous and justifies unfaithfulness to your spouse as long as sexual contact is avoided.

> Not only was he guilty of lusting after a woman to whom he had no right, but he was still such a klutz he hadn't even known how to pursue her. (*Left Behind*, p. 146)

Rayford was sorry for his misplaced lust, but on the other hand he was also sorry that he did not know how to take the action needed to bring this sin to the desired end. Rayford was too much of a klutz to know how to pursue Hattie? Why was a word with a negative connotation ("klutz") used in connection with marital fidelity? Why not say that Rayford was thankful to God that his moral restraints prevented him from taking the final, fateful step?

Prudes Are Faithful?

The following statement reveals the author's description of Rayford's moral code:

> He was no prude, but Rayford had never been unfaithful to Irene. (*Left Behind*, p. 3)

This is subtle, but the wording implies that there is a connection between being prudish or overly concerned with propriety if you are faithful to your spouse. This is clever wording that puts forth an undesirable message to the reader without his or her really being aware of it. When you read this type of sentence, you know that there is something strange about it, but you are not quite sure what. It does not sit well, but there is nothing terribly obvious that you can pinpoint, so you just go on with the book without finding out why this passage gave you reason to pause. *Left Behind* contains many such sentences, and you will read more about them in this book.

Adultery Is an Exciting Relationship?

> The question of the darkest hour before dawn, then, was whether Rayford Steele should risk a new, exciting relationship with Hattie Durham. (*Left Behind*, p. 4)

Adultery is being equated with being a new, exciting relationship. The fact that Rayford was not a Christian at the time the narrator was describing the situation in no way justifies painting adultery in such a positive light.

Speaking of light, because the darkest hour was when Rayford was trying to decide whether he should risk this "new, exciting relationship," the dawn is obviously the adulterous relationship itself. It is wrong to take such an insidious sin and present it in such a pleasing way.

"New, exciting relationship" and "dawn" have been chosen as synonyms for adultery. Do you really think that because this is a fictional book, it is acceptable to use positive words in connection with a sin that ensures the person who pursues it will not inherit the kingdom of God? The fact that it is fiction is not an excuse. Christians must not promote or defend anything that will cause someone to turn aside out of the way which the Lord has commanded (see Deut. 9:16).

Rayford and Hattie Did Not Yet Have a Relationship?

There is a very serious problem with the phrase "new, exciting relationship" in *Left Behind*. The authors painted Rayford's illicit relationship with Hattie, complete with clandestine dinner engagements, as though it was not *yet* a relationship, but could have become one. This is misleading because Rayford was *already* in a secret relationship with Hattie. It did not need to include sexual contact to qualify as a relationship:

> He had locked eyes with Hattie numerous times, and they had spent hours alone together over dinners in various cities. (*Left Behind*, p. 146)

The narrative about Hattie and Rayford conveys to the reader that a close, sexually charged, emotional connection between a man and woman not married to each other is not really a relationship, but only a potential one.

> "That's not it. Hattie, what's to cast aside? It's not like we had a relationship." (*Left Behind*, p. 278)

Here are two more examples of how the storyline conveys the message that Hattie and Rayford did not have a relationship of any kind because it had not proceeded to the point of becoming physically intimate:

> "I loved being with you and spending time with you. I found you beautiful and exciting, and I think you know I was interested in a relationship with you." (*Left Behind*, p. 369)

"I know we didn't really have anything going yet, but that would have been a kinder way to put it." (*Left Behind*, p. 370)

Time spent with Hattie did not constitute a relationship? The very real spiritual danger of what Rayford and Hattie were doing is being deliberately played down.

Lots of Time Spent in Secret With a Single Woman and Married Man Is Not Wrong?

The reader is being conditioned to believe that all this time spent together in secret between a single woman and a married man was not wrong. In a conversation with Rayford after he was saved, Hattie was trying to understand why Rayford had suddenly dumped her. She wanted to continue with the way things were in the past and said so:

"We could go back to the way things used to be, and except for what's in your mind there still wouldn't be anything wrong with it." (*Left Behind*, p. 279)

Here is the time where the newly converted Rayford should have told Hattie that the relationship was all wrong from the very beginning, including what he was thinking in his heart. Instead of using this dialogue to present biblical values, the authors actually put forth ungodly values through Hattie without countering them through Rayford. They should have had him gently correct Hattie and explain that it was wrong for her to touch him, flirt with him, and meet with him secretly, and that he was wrong to permit it. This should have been done so the reader would not be misled into justifying the same kind of sin in his own life.

Rayford and Hattie's Emotional Affair Is Not Wrong?

Rayford said, "If I had found you willing, I'd have eventually done something wrong." Hattie did not like to hear this, but Rayford continued. "Yes," he said, "it would have been wrong."

Continuing with the "we did not do anything wrong" theme, Rayford told Hattie,

> "But now I have to tell you how grateful I am that I didn't do something – well, stupid." (*Left Behind,* pp. 369-70)

Why did the authors use the conversation between Rayford and Hattie to persuade the reader that a romance between a married man and single woman isn't wrong as long as it doesn't degenerate to the point of sexual infidelity? The idea promoted throughout *Left Behind* is that as long as you do not reach the point of having intimate relations, some touching is not inappropriate; neither are surreptitious meetings to spend long hours talking with a person behind your spouse's back. This behavior went on between Rayford and Hattie, and he told her how grateful he was that they didn't do something stupid. They had a mutual attraction and they spent hours alone together, and yet this behavior was not lacking in judgment? This was not stupid behavior? I pray that the readers of *Left Behind* will not allow themselves to be led astray by these horrible examples.

Godly Sorrow Focuses Upon How We Have Offended God, Not Our Disgust With Ourselves

Rayford and Hattie's "almost-an-affair" would have been a good plot for the writers to teach the reader how wicked this sin is in the sight of God. But this was not to be. In a conversation with Chloe, Rayford reassured her that

> "The last thing on my mind is another woman, and certainly not Hattie." (*Left Behind,* p. 238)

The next sentence is instructive to the reader and the lesson falls far short of the Bible's standard:

> "She's too young and immature, and I'm too disgusted with myself for having been tempted by her in the first place." (*Left Behind,* p. 238)

Rayford expressed disgust with himself for being tempted by someone he now considered beneath him in maturity, rather than expressing to Chloe how sorry he was for having sinned against God and betraying his family's trust by engaging in a secret romance with Hattie.

Left Behind never addressed the issue of Rayford's mental adultery, which the Lord Jesus Christ defined as looking on a woman to lust after her, and thereby committing adultery with her already in his heart (see Matt. 5:28).

True repentance occurs when the sinner expresses remorse toward sinning against God and His holiness (with the commitment to forsake the sin), not merely disgust with himself for having committed that sin. The sinner who is truly repentant cares deeply about what God says about his sin, not merely what *he* thinks of it.

Many adulterers are disgusted with themselves for slipping back into this sin, but that does not mean they have turned toward God and called upon Him for salvation *from* their sin. This is an important difference. Being disgusted with sin is not enough to be saved. You must turn from your sins to the Lord Jesus Christ, who is the only one who has power on earth to forgive sins (see Matt. 9:6, Mark 2:10, Luke 5:24).

Rayford's Apology Did Not Address the Sin of Having a Romantic Relationship With Hattie

After Rayford came to faith in Christ, he wanted to seek out Hattie and apologize. He did not apologize for allowing himself to flirt with her, or accepting her physical affectionate gestures, or for meeting secretly with her behind his wife's back. Amazingly, the authors had this character apologize only because he did not sincerely love her, not because he wanted to engage in a physical relationship:

> "It isn't just that we're so far apart in age, but the fact is that the only real interest I had in you was physical." (*Left Behind*, p. 370)

He should have also told Hattie that he was sorry for pursuing her when he was married and had no right to allow their interactions to develop beyond the point of a professional working relationship. It was actually a romance, even though it had not degenerated into a sexual relationship. I suppose this would not have made sense in the story since the authors took such pains to put across the notion that a "relationship" did not describe what Rayford and Hattie were engaging in. But nevertheless it was a relationship, and it was clearly out of biblical bounds for a married man and should have been shown to be so in the story line.

God's Word on Adulterers

Among Christians, "fornication and all uncleanness must not be once named among you, as becometh saints" (see Eph. 5:3). There is definitely more than one time uncleanness is mentioned or named in *Left Behind*. Repeatedly the reader is shown that unfaithfulness to your spouse is not wrong as long as you do not plunge into a full-fledged sexual relationship.

> For by means of a whorish woman a man is brought to a piece of bread: and the adulteress will hunt for the precious life. (Prov. 6:26)

Even though Hattie made a point of touching Rayford when she had the opportunity, and Rayford accepted these gestures, this was made out to be an innocent act in the storyline. Whoever commits adultery receives a wound and dishonor, and a reproach that will not go away (see Prov. 6:33). Writers receive a reproach from God for using an emotional adulterous relationship as a subplot and making it seem much less serious than the Bible says it is.

The Bible says that adulterers will not inherit the kingdom of God, and that adultery as defined by the Lord Jesus Christ (who has the keys of hell and death) goes far beyond the commonly held definition of adultery. Jesus said, "But I say unto you, that whosoever looketh on a woman to lust after her hath committed adultery with her already in his heart" (Matt. 5:28). Jesus said that lusting after a woman is adultery committed in the heart. God will judge adulterers, and God will judge a fiction novel that makes light of mental adultery and depicts a single woman's expression of romantic affection towards a married man as being innocent. A novel that claims to be based upon the Holy Bible has no right to give the wicked example of a married man and a single woman spending hours alone together, and expressing through their dialogue that they did not have a relationship.

They had a relationship – an adulterous relationship as defined by God Himself – and if the reader follows *Left Behind's* lead and justifies Rayford and Hattie's sin, he will open a door for Satan to work in his own life in the same way. We must renounce the works of darkness, even darkness we have willingly taken into our minds through entertainment. The example of adultery being acceptable as long as it is not physical is antichrist and it is straight from Satan.

4

NICOLAE AND PRO-ABORTION PROPAGANDA

Nicolae has many examples of pro-abortion propaganda, and if you did not notice this when you read it, you are not alone. I did not notice it the first time I read *Nicolae,* even though I was reading it in an investigative manner, and I was on the alert for anything blatantly contrary to Christian doctrine or practice.

That was my problem. My antenna was tuned to pick up prominent antichrist teachings in the storyline. Propaganda is not effecttive if it is obvious, because it would be seen for the mind manipulation that it is and it would be rejected. Propaganda must be put to the recipient in such a way as to be received into the mind with as little resistance as possible.

The *Left Behind* series was written in such a way as to pervert major biblical truths, but because this is not easily seen, these perversions enter into the reader's mind without him even realizing it. It is similar to ingesting poison hidden inside a tasty-looking cake. The sugar masks the taste of the poison so it is easily swallowed. The evidence of the poison is not known until the person becomes sick.

In the case of the *Left Behind* series, the reader is not aware that he is absorbing spiritually poisonous teachings and examples because they are slipped into the story through deliberate wording that hides the actual messages being presented. *Nicolae* initially presents a Christian character dealing with the subject of abortion by having Rayford "plead his case against abortion without being too obvious." Why do the authors not want Christians to be obvious in presenting the Bible's teachings about killing an innocent baby, which is what abortion is all about? You will notice the "don't be too obvious about what God's Word says when dealing with the issue of abortion" theme repeating in the pages of *Nicolae*.

Rayford Conceded That Abortion Is an Option and a Solution

Let us look at how the authors had Rayford "not be too obvious" in his conversation with Hattie about her unwelcome pregnancy with Nicolae's child:

> "What do you think your options are?" (*Nicolae*, p. 294)

Rayford seemed to want to draw Hattie out in conversation so he brought up options. So far I am not objecting even to this question. There *are* options in the case where a woman finds herself unexpectedly pregnant: give birth to the baby and raise him, or give birth to the baby and give him a good home through adoption.

Hattie, of course, came up with three "options" and one was the "option" of abortion. She said,

> "And, of course, I can terminate the pregnancy." (*Nicolae*, p. 294)

Rayford replied:

> "You mean, have an abortion?"
> "Yes, what did you think I meant?"
> "Well, it just seems you're using language that makes it sound like the easiest option." (*Nicolae*, p 294)

This is a subliminal message inserted into the dialogue. Rayford, a Christian in the *Left Behind* series, conceded that abortion *is* an option. Hattie responded to this statement by saying,

> "It *is* the easiest option, Rayford." (*Nicolae*, p. 294) [italics in the original]

Rayford certainly pled his case without making it too obvious that he sided with God, didn't he? He agreed that abortion is an option by affirming that Hattie was making it sound like the *easiest* option. Abortion as an option was subtly confirmed by Rayford's statement, not denounced.

Later in the conversation, Rayford told Hattie that she had to make her own decisions about things, and commented that his opinion did not count much with her. Hattie replied,

> "Well, I care what you think. I respect you as someone who's been around. I hope you don't think that I think abortion is an easy decision, even though it's the best and simplest solution." (*Nicolae,* p. 295)

Rayford responded, "Best and simplest for whom?" The authors actually had Rayford concede that abortion is the best and simplest solution for *someone;* the question is for whom? The implication is that abortion is the best and simplest solution for the woman. This implication is reinforced as the dialogue continued with Hattie remarking that she needed to do something for Hattie, and since that did not turn out right, she now needed to do "something else" for Hattie:

> "Sometimes you have to look out for yourself. When I left my job and ran off to New York to be with Nicolae, I thought I was finally doing something for Hattie. Now I don't like what I did for Hattie, so I need to do something else for Hattie. Understand?" (*Nicolae,* p. 295)

This "something else" is abortion, and Rayford, making certain not to be "too obvious" in trying to persuade her against this decision, conceded that abortion *is* an option and that abortion is the best and simplest solution for someone. He was also guilty of hiding his light under a bushel, which is the opposite of Jesus Christ's command to His followers.

The authors should have had Rayford tell Hattie that abortion is *not* an option because God condemns killing, and they should have had Rayford say that abortion is *absolutely* not a solution for anyone, but they did not do this. Instead, they used this exchange to get across to the reader the pro-abortion propaganda that an abortion is an option for *someone* (the woman) and that it is the best and simplest solution for *someone* (the woman) through Rayford's dialogue with Hattie.

Abortion: For the Good of Hattie?

The dialogue between Rayford and Hattie continued along the theme of who benefits from an abortion. Hattie said,

> "When I left my job and ran off to New York to be with Nicolae, I thought I was finally doing something for Hattie. Now I don't like what I did for Hattie, so I need to do something else for Hattie. Understand?" (*Nicolae*, p. 295)

In keeping with the subtle pro-abortion propaganda theme, the authors used Rayford's thoughts to confirm the diabolical notion that abortion benefits a woman who is unhappily pregnant:

> He had to remind himself that Hattie was not a believer. She would not be thinking for the good of anyone but herself. Why should she? (*Nicolae*, pp. 295-96)

The authors inserted another subtle message in this narration: a woman wanting to have an abortion is thinking of the good of herself. Remember, this is narration. The authors are allowing the reader to know Rayford's thoughts on the matter. They should have had Rayford think that Hattie *thought* that an abortion would benefit her, but that she was deceived; but they did not do this. They had the choice of sending either a pro-life or pro-abortion message in the pages of *Nicolae*, and they chose the latter, though in a disguised manner.

No abortion benefits the woman having it, even if she feels immediate relief that her "problem" has been seemingly solved. David Reardon's book *Aborted Women, Silent No More* documents the after affects of abortions:

> ...the aftereffects of abortions... [with] complete testimonies of twenty aborted women... [and] a detailed national survey of 252 aborted women. Conservative Book Club [said] "It may be the most powerful book ever published on abortion."[1]

Abortions do have beneficiaries, however: They are Satan's followers, who push for abortion with all their might, (whether blatantly or subtly,) because they consider the deaths of these innocents to be a sacrifice to Satan himself.

Abortion is Justifiable in the Case of Rape or Incest?

Let us look at Rayford's attempts to dissuade Hattie from having an abortion and how the writers used their conversation to get across more seriously wrong messages to the reader:
Rayford told Hattie:

> "I'll even buy the argument that perhaps you regret the idea of having a child at all and would not be the best mother for it. I don't think you can shirk responsibility for it the way a rape or incest victim might be justified in doing." (*Nicolae*, p. 296)

Rayford told Hattie a rape or incest victim might be justified in having an abortion! "Shirking responsibility" is a euphemism for abortion in this context. Do you see how this value was slipped into the story in such a way that it is not obvious?

Rayford Says People Defend the "Right to Choose"

> "But even in those cases, the solution isn't to kill the innocent party, is it? Something is wrong, really wrong, and so people defend their right to choose." (*Nicolae*, p. 296)

The "right to choose" is treated as a fact, a given, in this sentence. Rayford used a pro-abortion buzz phrase and it slips right past the reader because the "something is wrong, really wrong" phrase precedes it and actually primes him to think that the rest of the sentence is a continuation of the pro-life words that precede it.

Something really *is* wrong, but that in no way makes "the right to choose" something that already exists. The "right to choose" may exist in the world that the Bible declares "lieth in wickedness" but it does not exist in the Word of God, and that is why it is terribly wrong to have a Christian character use pro-abortion rhetoric that abortionists use to try to justify abortion. The writers actually used a Christian character to promote pro-abortion propaganda, because Rayford did *not* say that God does not give us the "right to choose;" he said people defend this "right."

Straight Talk About Abortion's Killing Quality Is Going Too Far?

> Rayford had gone too far, and he had known it. He had glanced up at Hattie holding her hands over her ears, tears streaming down her face. He had touched her arm, and she had wrenched away. (*Nicolae*, p. 296-97)

Rayford told Hattie that pregnancy is the death of a person, and that the "most innocent party" of all is the one to be killed. The writers chose to show Rayford's frank (but not unkind) handling of abortion as an improper way to handle the situation. The message is that you must not be so straightforward about the deathly quality of abortion. You might offend somebody. Far more important, and not mentioned in the narration describing Rayford's thoughts, is that abortion offends God.

Rayford Asks Forgiveness for Insulting Hattie

Rayford apologized to Hattie because she was weeping and obviously quite offended with him for his straightforward stand on abortion:

> "I want you to forgive me for anything I said that hurt you personally or insulted you. I hope you know me well enough by now to know that I would not do that intentionally." (*Nicolae*, pp. 297-98)

Rayford said nothing insulting, and he was not unkind, which is essential when speaking the truth. Speaking the truth may be *taken* as an insult, but it is not insulting to speak the truth because the Lord Jesus Christ, who never sinned, spoke the truth – whether it created an offense or not – because the truth sets men free.

It would have been more acceptable if Rayford had said he was sorry if she felt insulted, but that is not the way the writers worded this sentence. Rayford asked forgiveness (which indicates that he felt he had wronged Hattie) for anything he said that hurt her or offended her. This example sends the message loud and clear that Christians are insulting a woman contemplating abortion if they are straightforward and tell her she would be killing an innocent child.

To *not* try to talk a woman out of an abortion is a serious sin of the silent, not-wanting-to-offend Christian. In fact, to keep quiet when your words are needed to help save not only the physical life of the baby but also the physical, spiritual, and emotional well-being of the mother is to be an accomplice to abortion.

Rayford Was Depicted as Mishandling His Talk With Hattie Because He Said Abortion Kills

Rayford was angry with himself. (*Nicolae*, p. 298)

Why would a Christian character be portrayed as being angry with himself for doing the will of God and declaring the hideous truth about abortion to a distraught woman about to make a tragic mistake that will not only destroy the child, but also damage her own soul?

> His motives were pure, and he believed his logic was right. But maybe he had counted too much on his own personality and style and not enough on God himself to work in Hattie's heart. (*Nicolae*, p. 298)

The Holy Spirit uses the Christian, an ambassador for Christ, to be salt and light to the inhabitants of this dark world, which lies in wickedness. Why did the authors seem to want to get across the opposite message to the reader?

> He may not have handled it the best way, but he knew trying to fix it now would accomplish nothing. (*Nicolae*, p. 299)

The only way to "fix" the way Rayford handled this situation would be to compromise and back off on any "thus saith the Lord" absolute truth stands. That is exactly how the authors had Chloe deal with Hattie later on: by compromise disguised as love.

Rayford's dialogue with Hattie exemplifies and reinforces the compromising "fear of man which bringeth a snare" rather than the Christ-like "Fear God and keep His commandments" (see Prov. 29:25, Ecc. 12:13).

Amanda Prayed for Wisdom to Share With Hattie

Before Amanda and Chloe conversed with Hattie, the group sat down to have a meal together. Amanda prayed and asked God to give them the words to minister to Hattie:

> "Give us words to say that might help her in whatever decision making she must do, and thank you for the provision of this food. In Jesus' name, Amen." (*Nicolae*, p. 375)

Take note of the fact that they asked God to give them words to speak to Hattie. This signals the reader to take seriously their example of "ministering" to Hattie, and to heed the words they spoke to her. Prayer was used throughout the *Left Behind* series as a propaganda technique to persuade the Christian reader to accept the example or doctrine to follow.

Rayford Gave Hattie the Right-Wing Position?

Hattie indicated to the group present at Loretta's house that her family had already encouraged her to have an abortion, and that she did want an abortion, but that she went to visit them because she knew they would try to talk her out of it:

> "I suppose I'm here because I know you'll try to talk me out of it, and I guess I need to hear both sides. Rayford already gave me the standard right-wing, pro-life position. I guess I don't need to hear that again." (*Nicolae*, p. 376)

The reader is being led to think that Rayford's indication that abortion might be justified on the basis of rape or incest is the standard pro-life position. This is amazingly bold pro-abortion propaganda. The pro-life position does not ever justify abortion in the cases of rape or incest. Abortion in and of itself destroys human life. The authors want the readers to think that abortion might be justified if the conception was due to rape or incest, and they even falsely connected these possible "exceptions" to the pro-life movement.

The female members of the Trib Force did not try to talk Hattie out of having an abortion. She actually stated that she wanted to be talked out of it, and that hearing both sides was the purpose of her visit, but the women saints did not try to do this. Instead, they offered her "love."

The only character who earnestly tried to talk Hattie out of having an abortion was Rayford, and the authors repeated twice that he was angry with himself for the way he handled the situation. They even had him apologizing for being up-front with the truth and wonder how much time he had to be diplomatic:

> ... *how much time is there to be diplomatic?"* (Nicolae, p. 297)
> [emphasis in the original]

Do you see how the right thing can be taught initially and then undone with a few strategically placed sentences? If being diplomatic or tactful means watering down the truth, then the answer is always, "There is no time to be diplomatic."

The Bible has the answers about how to speak to someone contemplating sin, and that is to speak the truth in love (Eph. 4:15) and let your speech be always with grace, seasoned with salt, "So that ye may know how ye ought to answer every man" (Col. 4: 6-7).

More Psychology-Based Pro-Abortion Rhetoric

Another bit of pro-abortion propaganda that must be mentioned here is that both Rayford and Buck were portrayed as not being qualified to advise Hattie about abortion because they were male. This is one of several examples of psychology and humanism manifesting their ugly heads in the series.

Here is some narration about Rayford's thoughts about Hattie's rejection to his pleas for her to protect her unborn child:

> "But he also knew she could reject it out of hand simply because he was a man. How could he understand? No one was suggesting what he could or could not do with his own body." (*Nicolae*, p. 297)

The authors also used Buck to reinforce the "men don't understand how women feel" pro-abortion rhetoric:

> "What do you need to hear?" Buck said, feeling very male and very insensitive just then." (*Nicolae*, p. 376)

> "Buck wanted to say something but he knew he couldn't communicate at this level." (*Nicolae*, p. 377)

What men can or cannot personally relate to has nothing to do with God's Word on abortion. Truth is truth no matter who is saying it or who is hearing it.

Nothing You Can Say Will Affect a Woman Considering an Abortion?

Chloe contradicted Hattie and told her she was not there to be talked out of having an abortion because she already knew where they stood on the matter. Then she told Hattie something that is a diabolical example to the Christian reader:

> "If you want to be talked out of it, we can do that. If you won't be talked out of it, nothing we say will make any difference." (*Nicolae*, p. 376)

What a terribly misleading lie. Many people active in pro-life work can tell you that a woman thinking of such a desperate measure wants and hopes to be talked out of it, and that many have indeed been talked out of it, much to the anger of those in the abortion industry. It is Satan (who considers each life taken in abortion a sacrifice to him) who would want to promote the lie that nothing said to a woman determined to abort will make any difference. What makes this example all the more devilish is the fact that prayer was offered to God for the right words and Satan's words were given in "answer" to this prayer.

Amanda told Hattie they would not preach to her because she already knew where they stood. Preaching, which is stating what God has already said in His Word, is made out to be the wrong tactic for a Christian to take in dealing with a woman desiring an abortion.

Abortion is Practical Advice?

Amanda went on to tell Hattie that something told her that her visit home was not successful:

> "Maybe they were too practical." (*Nicolae*, p. 377)

Advice to have an abortion is practical advice? Advice to have an abortion is useful? Useful to whom? Certainly not to the woman or the baby. But it is quite useful to Satan who derives much pleasure in the physical pain and emotional suffering he generates in the woman undergoing the abortion and by the excruciating pain inflicted upon the unborn being torn from the safety of his mother's womb.

Amanda went on to say,

> "Maybe they didn't give you the compassion you needed along with their advice." (*Nicolae*, p. 377)

The subtle communication here is that compassion can accompany the recommendation to get an abortion. A minority of people who promote abortion might feel this way because they are deceived, but these words were spoken by a Christian. This is the second time in this paragraph that positive words are being attached to the advice to have an abortion.

The "what do you want to hear" theme is repeated again when Amanda told Hattie:

> "Maybe hearing that they wanted you to end this pregnancy was not what you really wanted." (*Nicolae*, p. 377)

Reader, the antichrist message you are being sent is that you need to tell a woman with an unwanted pregnancy what she wants to hear. (Satan told Eve what she wanted to hear as well.)

Love Means Not Preaching Absolutes?

The passage I will cite next is one of the many antichrist ones in the *Left Behind* series. Yes, I am calling it antichrist because it is against absolute truth and therefore against the Lord Jesus Christ, whose name is Truth. The message about abortion presented in *Nicolae* is a message of non-absolutes in the place of absolute truth. Let us look at the following sentences and see how the Amanda character was used to get this idea across to the reader:

> "Let me just tell you, Hattie, if it's love you're looking for, you came to the right place." (*Nicolae*, p. 377)

The reader will now be instructed in what this Christian character is presenting as "love" to Hattie, a woman strongly leaning toward having an abortion:

> "Yes, there are things we believe. Things we think you should know. Things we think you should agree with. Decisions we think you should make. We have ideas about what you should do about your baby, and we have ideas about what you should do with your soul." (*Nicolae*, p. 377)

This passage is obviously soft-peddling God's absolutes and turning them into mere human opinion. A Christian character is turning a "thus saith the Lord" truth (the baby lives – period) into a "we *think* you should know and we *think* you should agree with," humanistic, compromising, "anti-absolute" stand. A Christian knows, not thinks he knows, what God says about the taking of innocent life.

This Christian character, who studies at the feet of Tsion, the Bible scholar, has mere *ideas* about what a pregnant woman desiring an abortion should do with her baby and her soul? It is not only God's Word on taking an innocent life that is being made relative here, but also His Word on salvation. More sickening, even sinister, is that this is all supposed to be representative of God loving Hattie through these Christians.

The next sentence gives the indication that these Christian characters will support and encourage Hattie no matter what decision she makes. God's Word is very clear on being an accomplice to evil, and supporting Hattie in this decision would be wicked, against love, and against God:

> "But these are personal decisions only you can make. And while they are life-and-death, heaven-and-hell decisions, all we can offer is support, encouragement, advice if you ask for it, and love. (*Nicolae*, p. 377)

According to this example, love is non-judgmental of actions that God's Word condemns. This is a destructive, antibiblical example. Christians are to be salt and light to the world whose deeds are evil.

What Should a Christian Do When Someone Is Making Heaven-and-Hell Decisions?

Chloe's statement to Hattie of support, encouragement, and advice only if requested also contained a hidden message to the reader that is anti-biblical and misrepresents the character of God:

> "And while they are life-and-death decisions, heaven-and-hell decisions, all we can offer is support, encouragement, advice if you ask for it, and love." (*Nicolae*, p. 377)

This statement was in regard to Hattie's choosing or not choosing to abort her unborn child. Now let us look at this message more closely:

1. If Hattie chooses not to kill her unborn baby, she will receive from these Christian women four things: support, encouragement, advice if she asks for it, and love.

2. If Hattie chooses to kill her unborn baby, these Christian women will offer her the same four

things: support, encouragement, advice if she asks for it, and love.

Make no mistake: the reader is being sent the message that in order to love the woman intent upon aborting her child, the Christian must support, encourage, and advise her only if she asks. To do these things is to show love, and not only love, but love the same way God loves. Hattie was skeptical of this statement:

> "Yeah," Hattie said, "love, if I buy into everything you have to sell."
> "No. We are going to love you anyway. We're going to love you the way God loves you." (*Nicolae*, p. 378)

That is a lie from the pit of hell. God never supports or encourages a sinner in his sin and He never overlooks sin and says, "I love you anyway." Any "God" who overlooks sin is a false "God" that cannot save. Holy and reverend is the name of the God who sent redemption to whoever will come to Him in repentance. The "God" that loves while the wicked do wickedly is not the God of the Holy Bible.

Removing the Last Abortion Deterrent: The Fear of God

This next section goes back to non-absolutes when referring to the abortion decision, and then swings over to absolutes whenever the false teaching of "God loves us no matter what we do" is mentioned. Let us look at this:

> "Even if your decisions go against everything we believe to be true, and even though we would grieve over the loss of innocent life if you chose to abort your baby, we won't love you any less." (*Nicolae*, p. 378)

> "We are not capable of unconditional love. That's why we have to let God love you through us. He's the one who loves us regardless of what we do. The Bible says he sent his Son to die for us while we were dead in our sins. That's unconditional love." (*Nicolae*, p. 378)

Chloe was assuring Hattie of God's love and acceptance *even if she chose the abortion*, thereby paving the way emotionally for Hattie to go through with an abortion. The reader is being fed the lie that this is God's way to minister to a woman thinking about having an abortion. This is not God's way, and pregnant women in crisis pregnancies really do want to be given a reason to protect both their babies' and their own lives. The book, *Aborted Women, Silent No More*, leaves an impact on me to this day. This book was filled with testimonies of women who felt alone and desperate when they discovered they were pregnant. Even so, they wanted – even yearned – for someone to speak out against abortion to them and to support them so they would have the resources and the courage to let the baby live. The stories about the heavy guilt they continued to carry for having given in to the pressure others exerted upon them to have an abortion are related in the book.

Much counsel and scriptural love (not counterfeit love) based upon the Word of God must be freely given to any woman victimized by abortion. It is wrong to give the go-ahead to the woman who has not yet had one by telling her that "God will love you anyway." This actually *facilitates* a decision for abortion by taking away what is usually the last deterrent: the fear of God.

This Is an Example of God Loving Through the Christian?

Hattie exclaimed that they could not love her if she ignored their advice. Let us remember that they gave her no advice. It was Rayford who "preached" and was made out by the authors to have mishandled the situation. Chloe was too busy "loving" Hattie, which in this book means refraining from preaching God's Word on the matter.

> Chloe agreed with her and told her "We are not capable of unconditional love. That's why we have to let God love you through us." (*Nicolae*, p 378)

God loving through a Christian is demonstrated in *Nicolae* to mean:
1. The Christian should tell the woman considering an abortion what she wants to hear; no absolute statements can be made (except to say God loves you regardless of what you do).
2. Not only should the Christian not speak out against abortion, but she should also use some positive words in connection with abortion.
3. The Christian should tell the woman she will be supported and encouraged in whatever decision she makes (this makes it so much easier for the woman to go ahead and get an abortion).
4. Last but not least, the Christian should reassure the woman that God loves her no matter what she does while she is thinking about aborting her unborn child.

"He's the one that loves us regardless of what we do."
(*Nicolae*, p. 378)

God Loves Us Unconditionally?

Chloe's statement about God sending His Son to die for us while we were dead in our sins does not mean that God's love is unconditional. Yes, the love that provided the means for whoever is willing come to Christ in faith and repentance to be rescued from the power and penalty of sin is completely undeserved:

> For when we were yet without strength, in due time Christ died for the ungodly. (Rom. 5:6)

We did nothing to merit God's love in sending Himself (in the person of His Son) to the cross to pay the price for our sins. However, Jesus did not die on the cross and come back to life on the third day to unconditionally love us while we continue to wallow in our sins. "Christ also hath once suffered for sins, the just for the unjust, that He might bring us to God" (see 1 Pet. 3:18).

Hattie is an unbeliever in *Nicolae*. The Holy Bible does not teach that an unbeliever is the recipient of God's unconditional love. Chloe, seeking to be "loving," did not quote God's Word, which, in fact, states the opposite:

> He that believeth on the Son hath everlasting life: and he that believeth not the Son shall not see life; but the wrath of God abideth on him. (John 3:36)

Hattie's state of unbelief means that the wrath of God, not His unconditional love, was *already* abiding upon her. A Christian character telling an unbelieving character that God unconditionally loves them even if they have an abortion is not true, and a snare to the reader. God not only judges the righteous, He is "angry with the wicked every day" (see Ps. 7:11).

Christians Must Keep Themselves in the Love of God

God's love is conditional to the believer and available to the unbeliever if he repents and calls upon the Lord Jesus Christ to be saved. God's love was for the purpose of reconciling us to Him, not to enable us to continue sinning while He unconditionally loves and forgives us. Salvation does *not* enable the person possessing it to continue sowing to the flesh and not reap the Bible's promised consequences of eternal corruption.

The Bible proclaims that Christians must keep themselves in the love of God (see Jude 1:21). What is this "love of God"? "That we keep His commandments" (see 1 John 5:31). This love is not unconditional, no matter what modern apostate theology may try to persuade you to believe, and no matter how many sinful examples of "Christianity" the *Left Behind* series contains.

The reconciled child of God is also a "crucified with Christ" child of God, and he must go on and live his life in the flesh in a particular way: "by the faith of the Son of God" who loved him and gave Himself for him (see Gal. 2:20). Those who live their lives by the faith of the Son of God (a holy life like Jesus lived by faith) and who understand their righteousness does not come by the Mosaic law are the ones who do not frustrate the grace of God.

Jesus Christ is not a minister of sin. The people who seek to be justified by Christ but are found to be sinners (they continue to practice sin) are treating Jesus as if He is a minister of sin (Gal. 2:17). God forbids this, and those who come to faith in the Lord Jesus Christ and then go back to rebuild a life of sin that faith in Christ had destroyed, are turning themselves into transgressors (Gal. 2:18).

To teach that God's love is unconditional is to deny the very character of God whose name is Holy; it is to lead people straight into hell where those who do not "repent and turn to God, and do works meet for repentance" will go to reap the wages of their sin (see Acts 26:20).

Buck Did Not Want to Raise Hattie's Baby

As I was reading this, I wondered why no Christian couple in the Trib Force offered to raise Hattie's baby. This would have been a beautiful example of how God's people could practically minister to women who were thinking of having abor-tions because they felt unable or unwilling to raise their babies.

Not only was this fine example not given, it was actually *taught against* in the storyline. Buck was hoping that Hattie would not have an abortion and that she would become a believer, but he certainly did not want to love his neighbor as himself and take the step of sacrifice needed to save the life of Hattie's baby:

> He tried to push from his mind that Chloe might get the idea of taking and raising as their own the unwanted baby Hattie was carrying. He and Chloe were close to a decision about whether to bring a baby into this stage of history, but he hardly wanted to consider raising the child of the Antichrist. (*Nicolae*, pp. 383-84)

Every baby is worth saving, because every baby conceived is made in the image of God, no matter who the father may be. Refusing an abortion also saves the mother a lifetime of remorse.

Putting self first, ahead of saving the life of an innocent baby, is a reprehensible example. Jesus said that every man who comes after Him *must* deny himself, take up his cross, and follow Him (see Mark 8:34).

Choosing to bring up the subject of abortion in the *Left Behind* series was a prime opportunity for the authors to proclaim to the entire world God's *absolute Word* on the matter of the taking of human life. The authors declined to do this, but instead subtly, and sometimes not so subtly, interjected pro-abortion propaganda into the storyline. They drew the reader along to empathize with the woman contemplating abortion rather than focusing the reader on God's absolute Word on the matter.

Abortion was promoted in the story through well-disguised, politically correct propaganda. This serves not the Christian community with examples of godliness and conformity to God's Word, but rather the purposes of the New World Order. Even now they are using abortion and forced abortion to slow down population growth, and they will use this as one of their means to reduce the world's population by huge numbers in the time to come.

5

CHILD MURDER AND SUICIDE: OPTIONS FOR CHRISTIANS DURING THE TRIBULATION?

> The thief cometh not, but for to steal, and to kill, and to destroy: I am come that they might have life, and that they might have it more abundantly. (John 10:10)

Chloe's plans to kill her son and then herself is a rather obvious antichrist subplot. In this chapter, you will see how the authors further reinforced this diabolical subplot through the characters' thoughts and dialogue. Chloe was studying, and Tsion commended her for her diligence until she stopped him and told him the focus of her studies:

> "I've been studying death." Tsion narrowed his eyes. "I'm listening."
> "I will not allow myself or my baby to fall into the hands of the enemy." (*The Indwelling*, p. 56)

There is no mention here or anywhere in the series of seasons of fasting and prayer for Kenny's protection, but we *do* learn that Chloe was studying behind her husband's back to learn of a quick and accurate way to murder her own son and to commit self-murder afterwards:

> "I will not allow Kenny or me to fall into their hands."
> "And how will you ensure this?"
> "I would rather we were dead."
> "You would kill yourself."
> "I would. And I would commit infanticide."
> She said this with such chilling conviction that Tsion hesitated, praying silently for wisdom. "Is this a sign of faith or lack of faith?" he said finally. (*The Indwelling*, p. 57)

Tsion's Prayer Revealed Wisdom From God?

Right after Chloe revealed her plan to Tsion, he prayed for wisdom about how to answer her. This character, a Bible scholar, could not think of anything more to say to a Christian woman intent upon murdering her own son and then herself than, "Is this a sign of faith or lack of faith?" Tsion knew the Bible thoroughly and definitely would have known that Chloe's premeditated plan to murder her child was edging her dangerously close to drawing back unto perdition rather than believing to the saving of her soul (see Heb. 10:39). Chloe was determined to commit a deed that was a departure from the Christian faith and Tsion did not admonish her biblically except to use the weak phrase above and some psychological mind games.

Sinning "Helps" God Keep Us Safe?

Chloe's response to Tsion's question about faith teaches the reader another anti-Christian message:

> "I don't know, but I can't imagine God would want me or my baby in that situation." (*The Indwelling*, p. 57)

The message here is that you should take matters into your own hands to keep yourself safe during the tribulation. Since the *Left Behind* series teaches eternal security of the non-overcoming kind, it follows that "anything goes" for a Christian, and this is a prime example of this unbiblical teaching. Chloe based her decision to kill her son and herself on her imaginings that God would not want her to end up in that situation (which is true). But rather than rely upon God Himself who has given unto us *all things* that pertain unto life and godliness (even during the tribulation), she made her own carnal, "sin unto death" plans to take care of herself and her son (see 2 Pet. 3).

It was a serious soul-subverting ploy for the authors to insert into the story the scenario of a Christian planning to do such a faithless deed and *leave out* Bible answers to what could be a very real dilemma in the time to come. Tsion Ben-Judah, her spiritual mentor, was filled with all knowledge of scripture, but he never opened the Bible with her, never quoted any scripture, and never told her she must repent. He never even offered to pray with her at the close of the conversation.

Sadly, ungodly examples are the norm rather than the exception in the *Left Behind* series. The characters are not called to glory and virtue in the practical out-working of their faith, which is the only faith that is of the Christian kind. They are called to mere intellectual ascent to certain facts about Christ. This did not result in them walking in newness of life, but instead, brought them a life of fear, deceptive ploys, and hypocrisy to try to save their own lives in this world.

Rayford and Tsion Sympathized With Chloe's Murderous and Faithless Feelings

Rayford was heartsick that Chloe was so determined to kill Kenny rather than see him fall into the hands of the enemy. And yet as a father, he could identify with her passion. It terrified him that she had thought it through to the point where she had an injection prepared. (*The Indwelling*, p. 312-13)

These are the thoughts the authors chose for Rayford to have about Chloe's murder plans for Kenny. They did not portray Rayford as being heartsick that Chloe did not have faith to trust God to protect Kenny; instead, they chose to have him convey sympathy.

If the writers adhered to the plain teachings of the Holy Bible and the most holy faith, they would have had Rayford be grieved that Chloe was embarking on the broad road of destruction by contemplating murder. They would have had him do the biblical thing and *confront* Chloe and warn her that murderers shall have their part in the lake which burns with fire and brimstone (see Rev. 21:8). The Bible teachings the authors left out of the storyline are almost as damaging as the false teachings they put into it.

Tsion was also depicted as having sympathy for Chloe's gross lack of faith in God to care for her and her baby during perilous times:

> "That you would be sympathetic, at least."
> "I am that, at the very least." (*The Indwelling,* p. 59)

It is ominous the authors chose to have sympathy expressed for Chloe twice in this exchange, thus reinforcing the message. Also, notice that Tsion said that he was sympathetic "at the very least." The message to the reader is: The least you can do is be sympathetic to the notion that Christians may become so desperate during the tribulation that they may decide to kill their own family members and even themselves to escape the stress of living by faith in perilous times.

Why Chloe and the Rest of the Trib Force Did Not Have Faith That Jesus Would Keep Them from Evil During The Tribulation

Chloe was so petrified that Kenny would fall into the hands of the GC that she formulated a plan to instantly kill him should the enemy ever invade the safe house. This is an example of walking by sight and not by faith. The Bible teaches that Christians must walk by faith and not by sight (2 Cor. 5:7), yet we see the Trib Force walking by sight most of the time in the *Left Behind* series. Why?

The reason they did not walk by faith is because they were not living by the faith of the Son of God, which is a "dead to self and alive unto God" kind of life. They did not identify with Jesus and consider themselves dead to sin and alive in Him. They merely "knew about" Jesus and wanted Him to take them to heaven, but they knew nothing of real Christianity, and thus were merely "head-knowledge" Christians which are of the going-to-hell-kind. They did not surrender in faith to the real Lord Jesus Christ, which is the only kind of Christianity the Bible teaches.

The Trib Force did *not* walk in obedience to God's commands, and so Chloe's confidence of God's protection was severely lacking, and rightfully so. Their lack of faith that they would be kept from evil during the tribulation was warranted. Why? Because they did not meet the condition to receive Jesus' promise of protection, which was to be "not of the world," even as Jesus was not of this world. Jesus' prayer was that His "sanctified by the truth" disciples would be protected in tribulation (see John 17:15-19). Chloe and the rest of the Tribulation Force "believed" the truth but they were not sanctified through this truth (this is true salvation), and therefore lived like the world. And as you can see in this example, they were being overcome by the world.

In Perilous Times Make Provision for the Sins of the Flesh?

Chloe committed the horrible sin of planning to kill her son and herself rather than pray unceasingly and trust God to protect them. This is an outrageous and soul-subverting example for anyone reading the books – either the non-Christian or the Christian. The unbeliever sees yet another example of "Christians" in the Trib Force sinning as a lifestyle in order to survive during the tribulation, and the Christian sees this presented as a possible solution if the situation becomes exceedingly dangerous during the tribulation.

The authors' depiction of Chloe making provision for this heinous sin and Rayford's identification with her feelings of passion toward "protecting" Kenny by killing him are bad enough. But the most serious doctrinal problem taught through this fictional situation is that the authors did *not* have Tsion, the spiritual leader and mentor of the group, rebuke her actions as a soul-damning sin as taught in the Holy Bible. Nor was there any mention of Tsion taking the lethal injection and disposing of it when Chloe left the safehouse, which is what any Christian would have done in good conscience, considering her determination to actually commit murder.

Psychological Argumentation Replaces the Sword of the Spirit

Tsion attempted to talk Chloe out of murdering Kenny and herself by using *psychological tactics* rather than scriptural admonitions:

> "Then it follows that Cameron would be justified in killing himself."
> She bit her lip and shook her head. "The world needs him."
> "The world needs you, Chloe. Think of the co-op, the international—"
> "I can't think anymore," she said. "I want done with this! I want it over! I don't know what we were thinking, bringing a child into this world." (*The Indwelling*, p. 59)

Tsion continued with his emotional, but definitely not scriptural, pleas:

> "That child has brought so much joy to this house –" Tsion began.
> Chloe responded: "– That I could not do him the disservice of letting him fall into GC hands."
> Tsion sat back, glancing at the TV. "So the GC comes, you kill the baby, kill yourself, Cameron and your father kill themselves...when does it end?" (*The Indwelling*, p. 59)

In keeping with his psychological manipulation rather than standing upon the word of God, Tsion even went so far as to imply that he would commit suicide too:

> "Neither do I want to live without you and the little one. You know what comes next." (*The Indwelling*, p. 59)

It is easy to see where the authors went with this scenario. There is not one word from Tsion, the biblical scholar and spiritual mentor of the Tribulation Force, about what the Holy Bible teaches about murder and about how close Chloe is coming to departing from the faith. Tsion never sternly rebuked and warned Chloe that no murderer has eternal life abiding in her, and that if she murders Kenny or murders herself she will have her part in the lake that burns with fire and brimstone. This place is for the unbelieving, the fearful, and the murderers, which the authors had a Christian character commit to becoming.

Chloe's Instructions for the Way She Wanted Kenny to Be Murdered: Decisive and Sure

Chloe was so determined that Kenny must die if the GC got to the cellar where Tsion would be hiding with Kenny that she begged Tsion to promise her he would do the deed if they showed up when she was gone:

> "You have to promise me, Tsion, please! Under my mattress is a syringe with a potassium chloride solution. It'll work quick, but you have to inject it directly into his buttocks. You can do it right through the diaper. It doesn't have to be perfect; it just has to be decisive and sure." (*The Indwelling*, p. 308)

Kenny's murder did not have to be executed in a *perfect* way, only in a *decisive* and *sure* way. See the little print subliminal inserted into the dialogue? Decisive, sure, and perfect are all words with positive connotations. There is a pattern throughout the *Left Behind* series in that the authors use positive words in connection with sinful actions (see Chapter 3). The use of wording in this manner makes the text work as a print subliminal.

The authors should have used negative words to describe such a wicked and faithless act: "You don't have to stab him in an exact spot. You just have to direct the poison directly into his buttocks' muscle." (See Chapter 2 for examples of propaganda techniques.) They could have worded it a number of different ways that did not slip any positive words into the description of how Kenny's life was to be extinguished. The words "decisive and sure" sound almost noble, and do not belong in the description of a premeditated infanticide.

Tsion refused to murder the baby boy, and promised Chloe he would protect Kenny to his fullest capability. As Chloe was leaving the safe house he told her,

> "God is with us." (*The Indwelling*, p.308)

But Tsion never warned her of the *eternal* consequences of murdering her child and herself! Because this warning was left out, the reader will think that to be a Christian is to be able to commit any sin – even murder – as long as he has a good rationalization for it. This message is anti-biblical and antichrist.

Murder and Suicide Subplot Handled in a Doctrinally Deceptive Manner

What Rayford and Tsion did *not* say to Chloe in this situation speaks even more loudly to the reader than what they did say to her. Chloe is a fictional character and thus her soul is not real and she cannot be harmed by not being told that she was on the verge of departing from the faith.

The reader, however, *is* real and *does* have a soul, and is receiving the message that killing her child to keep him from Antichrist's people is something that a Christian might feel the need to resort to in the times ahead. This message is coming from a book series allegedly "hung upon a scriptural outline." Furthermore, the reader is shown that making a decision like this has no effect upon his or her salvation.

After all, none of the characters privy to Chloe's plans condemned them as a hell-sending ones, did they? No, they did not. Tsion even promised to keep Chloe's plans from Buck. *Left Behind's* theme of holding the truth in unrighteousness extends to the degree that even murder and self-murder are actions a Christian can get away during the tribulation. Yes, the "you are more than a conqueror through Him that loved you *even while you are being overcome by sin"* theme is strongly promoted by Chloe's faithless, fearful, and murderous example.

This is not a true depiction of Christianity. It is a "holding the truth in unrighteousness" kind of Christianity, which is of the apostate kind. The fictional scenario of a Christian planning the murder of her own child and herself and never receiving any scriptural rebuke and never repenting of planning such a deed is an abomination and a disgrace to true Christianity. The Bible is clear that if we confess our sins, God is faithful and just to forgive us our sins. The authors never had Chloe confess her sin of planning to kill Kenny. This is one of many examples of false Christianity in the series.

Chloe's example also teaches that God cannot be trusted to protect his own children during the upcoming period of time known as the tribulation, and that God's people might have to resort to the desperate measures of those lost and without Christ in this world. The example this is setting and the thoughts this is implanting in the minds of millions is downright evil.

> There hath no temptation taken you but such as is common to man: but God is faithful, who will not suffer you to be tempted above that ye are able, but will with the temptation also make a way to escape, that ye may be able to bear it.
> (1 Cor. 10:13)

If the authors wanted to depict Chloe as a true Christian, they would have provided her with a way to bear her uncertainties concerning the GC. She would not have given into fear, which is the opposite of faith.

This subplot should have been used to teach sound doctrine instead of doctrines of devils which lead people away from the true Christian faith. (see 1 Tim. 4:1) In order to teach sound doctrine the authors should have had Tsion tell Chloe the truth: murderers do not inherit the kingdom of God. Tsion should have exhorted Chloe to "continue in the faith." She should have been told that believers will go through much tribulation before they enter into the kingdom of God" (Acts 14:22). Why wasn't the "murder and suicide" subplot handled scripturally as a godly lesson for the reader instead of being used as a spiritually destructive snare?

Soul-Damning Message in the "Chloe Plans to Kill Kenny" Storyline

Chloe's determination to take the life of her son and commit self-murder was dismissed without any show of remorse or repentance toward God for siding with Satan instead of Him in this situation. We did not hear about it later except when Leah asked whether Chloe had learned how to make the solution from her medical books.

This situation was never resolved biblically in the story, so the reader is definitely left with the lie that a true Christian should not kill his child or himself because it would upset other people, but not because he would forfeit his own soul. Therefore, if you can handle the fact that other people would be distraught, you can kill your children and yourself to escape Antichrist's regime. You will not go to hell, and can therefore be a Christian and a murderer (and self-murderer). This false teaching states that once you make the decision for Christ, the blood of Jesus will cleanse you of all sin even if you do not confess your sins and even if you do not walk in the light as He is in the light (see 1 John 1:7-9). This is the actual message in the "Chloe planning to kill Kenny" subplot in *The Indwelling*.

Will a Christian Who Commits Suicide Go to Heaven?

"Yes," according to the message in *The Indwelling*, and "No" according to the Word of God. Suicide is really *unbelief* that God is able to make a way of escape from a temptation "common to man" and unbelief that God is willing and able to make an escape from self-murder so that we can bear the temptation without succumbing to it. Suicide is rebellion against God by terminating a life that He created to bring glory to Himself.

A Christian who commits suicide dies not in faith that God can take care of him in spite of his misery, but in unbelief, rebellion and utter despair. It is literally dying in unbelief. Emotional pain is usually the catalyst for a Christian to become very offended with God for not fixing things in his life to the point where he feels they are endurable. Most Christians have probably felt at some point that life is so unbearable that they wish they would just die and go to be with the Lord. True Christians are strangers and pilgrims in this world; it is not their home – even more so during the tribulation when the world will be completely run by Satan's human agents.

God's people, who are called to be holy, must not learn the way of the heathen and resort to killing themselves under extreme duress with the assumption they will be carried to heaven. Christians have been bought with a price and are commanded to glorify God in their body and in their spirit, which are God's (1 Cor. 6:20). The Bible says that whoever is born of God overcomes the world, and the victory that overcomes the world is our faith (see 1 John 5:4). We must purpose to continue in the real Christian faith, which truly does overcome the world. We must not conform to the world the way Chloe did in *The Indwelling*. We must not succumb to Satan as he seeks to steal, kill, and destroy our faith through the guise of Christian fiction.

Suicide is Satan's eternal "solution" to Christians who become seriously offended in Christ. That is why Christians must consciously reject this sin unto death long before he is tempted to commit it. The time is approaching when there will be many Christians worldwide who will be greatly offended in Christ when the tribulation begins in earnest. They will find that they have not been raptured as their teachers promised, but Jesus Himself never promised this. These Christians must not have thoughts in the back of their minds that they have a way out through suicide, because this is the *opposite* of overcoming and the *opposite* of faith in Jesus. They will not inherit eternal life if they violate the conditions set in the word of God for His own people bought with the blood of Christ, which is to stand fast, overcome, and continue in Jesus' word. Please, whatever your eschatological beliefs may be, purpose in your heart right now that you will not lose faith in Christ and fall into despair. The Lord Jesus Christ will keep you as you stand firm in faith under pressure and endure to the end.

Commit Your Soul Unto God: He Is Faithful

If we have to suffer, let it be *only* according to the will of God, and not the will of Satan, who would love to have us reap corruption if he can cause us to believe his lies over the Holy Bible. He hopes that we will forfeit God's free gift by believing his lie that faith can be held in unbelief, fear, murder, adultery, fornication, drunkenness, thievery, covetousness, malice, envy, idolatry, and other sins. The apostle Paul warned Christians that those who *do such things* will not inherit the kingdom of God (see 1 Cor. 6:9-10, Gal. 5:21, Eph. 5:5).

Yes, in tribulations now and in the tribulation to come we will suffer as Christians because we live on a battlefield, but we must determine to suffer only according to the will of God, and not according to the will of Satan. The Tempter constantly plots against us, hoping that we will to succumb to the temptation to sin so we will put ourselves outside of God's protection. This is what it means to suffer according to the will of Satan.

We must commit the keeping of our souls to God in well doing, as unto a faithful Creator, which He truly is (see 1 Pet. 4:19). Whatever we suffer for His sake, He is surely able to keep that which we have committed to Him against that day if we will only hold fast the form of sound words which are written in the Holy Bible, and hold fast to faith and love which is in Christ Jesus (see 2 Tim. 1:12,13).

6

DISAPPEARANCES: THE BEST-KEPT SECRET

The manner in which the authors depicted the aftermath of the disappearances is ominous indeed. Even more disturbing is that the authors' depiction of the happenings at the outset of the tribulation parallel what is actually *planned* by the New World Order elitists. The authors depicted the disappearances as being "reports of death and destruction," (*Left Behind*, p. 46), a "tragedy," "the most shocking event of history" (*Left Behind*, p. 209), "an unusually horrific season in history" (*Left Behind*, p. 273), "a nightmare" (*Left Behind*, p. 274), "a crisis" (*Left Behind*, p. 353), and more terrifying descriptive phrases.

> "If Bruce Barnes was right, the disappearance of God's people was only the beginning of the most cataclysmic period in the history of the world." (*Left Behind*, p. 343)

There will be mass disappearances around the world that might be reported by the media as occurring simultaneously, but they will not occur because Jesus Christ has taken His people from the earth in a secret, pre-tribulation rapture that He never promised. The horrific happenings the authors portrayed as being caused by Jesus rapturing His people from the earth before the tribulation is without any scriptural foundation.

It is not in the character of the true God of the Holy Scriptures to prove to a rebellious, disobedient world that He performs His Word. It *is* in God's character to prove His own people, and if they prove and do what is acceptable to Him, He will allow them to prove Him (see Deut. 13:3, Ps. 26:2, Mal. 3:10).

The *Left Behind* series gives an anti-biblical impression to the reader that God will change character and give a sign to prove to an unbelieving world that His Word is true. Jesus said this will not happen:

> But he answered and said unto them, "An evil and adulterous generation seeketh after a sign; and there shall no sign be given to it, but the sign of the prophet Jonas." (Matt. 12:39)

Signs do not change hard-hearted, mocking hearts:

> He saved others; himself he cannot save. If he be the King of Israel, let him now come down from the cross, and we will believe him. (Matt. 27:42)

The authors devised a plot that made certain evidences, which can be reproduced by man, proof that the rapture of the church had truly happened. The Lord Jesus Christ did not say He would return twice; He said He would return immediately after the tribulation. (see Matt. 24:29) The Lord does not approve of anyone who says He said something would come to pass when He did not say it:

> To turn aside the right of a man before the face of the most High,
> To subvert a man in his cause, the LORD approveth not.
> Who is he that saith, and it cometh to pass, when the Lord commandeth it not? (Lam. 3:35-37)

Disappearances: A Trigger Word Meant to Trigger an Automatic Response

The *Left Behind* writers have taken the words "disappear," "disappearances," and "disappeared" and actually created for them a theological meaning with a jarring emotional impact upon the hearer. A version of the word "disappear" appears more than 60 times in *Left Behind* alone.[1] Occasionally the word "vanishings" was used, but the word that has been used so often that it qualifies as a trigger word is "disappearances," or a form of it.

"Disappearances" is really a buzzword or trigger word:

> Buzzwords are words which impart strong emotional responses and all sorts of sensational images and ideas. Buzzwords are created by conditioning by repetitive association and usually convey negative

connotations and images. Buzzwords are an economic way of conveying propaganda.[2]

The word "disappearances" and its variations definitely qualify as buzzwords because they are being used to condition the reader to respond automatically when he hears them mentioned in a particular context. The conveying of automatic responses or feelings is exactly what the repetitious use of the word "disappearances" is accomplishing in *Left Behind*. The reader is inundated with this word and is being conditioned to have an automatic, rather than reasoned response when he reads or hears the word "disappearances" in connection with people being missing. He will bypass analytic thinking because this word will trigger in him an overwhelming emotional response.

This conditioning will cause him to act on the response programmed into his mind and he will think, "Jesus raptured His church and I have been left behind," or, "My faith is phony, I'm not a true Christian," or even, "Was Jesus *really* the Christ, or should I look for another?" This kind of reaction would cause many to fall away from the faith of the true Lord Jesus Christ. What is even more sobering is that Antichrist's Globalist regime will be delighted to help the devastated "left behind" Christian look for another "Christ." They will lead him straight to the "Coming One," or "Maitreya," as they call him.

When repetition is used to teach something, The Credibility Factor comes into play:

> The Credibility Factor is a phenomenon in which a subject is given credibility in proportion to the degree to which it is propagated.[3]

The teaching that disappearances means the rapture was made much more credible in the storyline by repetition, scripture citations, and depictions of televised broadcasts in which "live coverage" of disappearances in progress was made out to be irrefutable proof that the rapture of the church had actually happened.

Christians Will Not Snatched Away By an Evil Force?

The *Left Behind* series sends the message that if you hear about mass disappearances you should not suspect that any foul play has occurred. This message was dispensed on Pastor Billings' videotape, thereby giving it more authority to the reader:

> "Let me encourage you that your loved ones, your children and infants, your friends, and your acquaintances have not been snatched away by some evil force or by some invasion from outer space. That will likely be a common explanation. What sounded ludicrous to you before might sound logical now, but it is not." (*Left Behind,* p. 212)

The last sentence is manipulatively written, but if we examine it carefully the message is plain. Pastor Billings said, "What sounded ludicrous to you before." What would have sounded ludicrous before? The idea that a loved one, friend, or acquaintance could be snatched away by an evil force. Look at the trickiness here. Pastor Billings said it might sound logical now (the idea that ones loved ones could be snatched away by an evil force) but it is not.

The authors had Pastor Billings communicate that it is not logical for a Christian to think their loved ones could have been snatched away by an evil force or by some invasion from outer space. Certainly an invasion from outer space is far fetched. However, Christian loved ones, friends, and acquaintances could definitely be snatched away by evil people, and Jesus said this would happen. (See Mat. 24:9).

The fact that most churches are registered with the government with the members' names and addresses on file actually makes it easy for Christians to be found and snatched away by evil people when the New World Order wants all dissenters eliminated We must come to terms with the truth that the New World Order will not be instituted in peace, but in brute force, *against* those who refuse to "go along with the program."

The Only Logical Explanation Is God?

The *Left Behind* storyline conditions the reader to discount the possibility that there could be another explanation for mass disappearances:

> Rayford calculated that the disappearances would have taken place late evening, perhaps around 11 P.M. central time. Would anything have taken them away from home at that hour? He couldn't imagine what, and he doubted it. (*Left Behind*, p. 64)

If mass disappearances of Christians were to occur in the middle of the night, should nobody wonder or investigate, but automatically and without conscious thought, assume that they were taken in the air by the Lord?

> "Buck's eyes were watering. "Yeah, sure, but what was that you said about rapture?"
> "Is there any other explanation that makes sense?" the doctor said, using a scalpel to tear into Buck's hair. (*Left Behind*, p. 60)

> Few people who sat under the earnest and emotional teaching of Bruce Barnes could come away doubting that the vanishings had been the work of God. (*Tribulation Force*, p. 60)

Yes, there *is* another explanation that makes sense for seemingly simultaneous mass disappearances of Christians.

No Other Logical Explanation for Missing Persons?

The "no other explanation" theme is repeated in *Left Behind*. This theme is to convince the reader to believe that if a person is missing and his clothes remain where the "left behind" person can find them, the explanation is the rapture. There is no other logical explanation.

Remember that buzzwords are used so that the people hearing them do not think rationally, but only react according to the manner in which they have become accustomed to thinking about that word. The same "don't think of every possible scenario, just react on cue" propaganda technique is being set forth with the "no other logical explanation" theme. Here are some examples of where this is used in *Left Behind*:

> "You're saying the only logical explanation is God, that he took his own and left the rest of us?"
> "That's what I'm saying." (*Left Behind*, p. 165)

Here is another time the authors plugged the "no other explanation" notion to the reader:

> There was no other explanation for the two witnesses in Jerusalem. Nor for the disappearances. (*Left Behind*, p. 440)

The authors went so far as to portray a person who believed there could be another explanation for the disappearances as not wanting to admit that it was really God:

> And to people who didn't want to admit that God had been behind the disappearances, any other explanation would salve their consciences. (*Left Behind*, p. 344)

The characters in *Left Behind* did not investigate all possible reasons for the disappearances, and the people who questioned the "rapture reason" were depicted as skirting around the issue of dealing with God.

Rayford angrily said to his "disbelieving in the rapture theory" daughter,

> "What's more far-fetched than people disappearing right out of their clothes? Who else could have done that?" (*Left Behind*, p. 164)

Who else indeed? The answer to that question has been known a long time by those involved with implementing The Plan.

Disappearances: The Real, Modern-Day Meaning

"Disappearances" has a real, present-day meaning. It means the forced abduction of people, whether of a few, or of thousands, who are never to be heard from again. Mass worldwide disappearances are an integral part of The Plan to bring in the new global order of Antichrist. This fact is virtually unknown to those not directly involved in this plan, and it is being deliberately kept from Christians, Jews, and patriots, against whom The Plan is specifically directed.

There are many words that are directly related to disappearances. All of them are ominous: detention, imprisonment, intimidation, abduction, missing, persecutions, reprisals, violations, harassment, death, killings, torture, military police, physical abuse, beatings, rape, detention centers, and more.[4]

In various countries the military has been the cause of the often unexplained disappearances of thousands of people:

> For decades the evidence of military involvement is strong, especially since in many of the cases, the kidnappers either picked their victims up from district military commands or took them from a kind of safehouse where they were held to police or military commands in Jakarta. The failure of the military fact-finding team to come up with any facts after almost two months suggests a deliberate decision to keep the truth hidden.[5]

Armed forces have been involved in detaining the "missing." Many of the "disappeared" are political activists or dissidents who have been at odds with military takeovers and the loss of human rights. Disappearances have been ordered in the past, are being ordered presently, and will be ordered *en masse* in the future when the New World Order begins in earnest.

For examples of past disappearances, see the article, "Twentieth Century Atlas – Death Tolls."[6] Here you will find a long list of countries where dictators seized control and caused mass disappearances of multitudes of people. For example, from 1957-1986, Papa Doc Duvalier was the dictator of Haiti. Under his cruel regime, 15,000 people disappeared, while over 150,000 were killed.

When governments are responsible for kidnapping and killing their own citizens, they are committing democide, or "death by government." Governments kill their own citizens according to a carefully researched pattern:

> We can say from Table 22.1 that the dominant pattern of democide, that centrally involving domestic democide, is exclusively

related to patterns of total and political power on the one hand and the likelihood of rebellion against a regime.[7]

This will be precisely the case when the New World Order is implemented on a global scale. Those known to be likely to rebel against the new regime will be eliminated by their own government. Who would be considered to be at enmity with the new regime? Christians and Jews.

> An important part of The Plan is to eliminate Christians and Jews, the natural enemies of the New World Order.[8]

As you can see from this brief look at modern-day disappearances, "disappearing" has been going on for a long time. Because the same reasons for the past disappearances will exist again, the disappearances will occur again. But this time, the disappearances will be on a global scale.

The Plan: Destroy and Eject

Nicolae Carpathia spoke positively to Buck about the disappearances:

> "But it took the vanishings – which may have been the best thing that ever happened to this planet – to finally bring us together."
> (*Tribulation Force*, p. 128)

This happens to be an accurate depiction of how the leaders of the New World Order will view the worldwide disappearances of Christians. They are the people who will be ordering and overseeing the elimination of all who refuse to accept the propaganda that has been used to prepare them to become citizens in the New Age.

Alice Bailey, in an address at the Arcane School Conference in Geneva, Switzerland, suggested that the "Shamballa force" – the force from the invisible dimensions led by the Lord Maitreya – will be destructive:

> "It will also," she said, "eject unbelievers from the earth: The decision to release the Shamballa force during this century into direct

contact with the human kingdom is one of the final and most
compelling acts of preparation for the New Age. The Shamballa force
is destructive and ejective ... inspiring new understanding of The
Plan. It is this force, which will bring about that tremendous crisis,
the initiation of the race into the mysteries of the ages."[9]

It has long been The Plan to eject unbelievers – any person who refuses to be initiated into the New Age and accept its False Christ – from the earth. This ejection from the earth will send Christians into another dimension, which is the occult euphemism for death:

All types of OBEs (out of body experiences) demonstrate that
there is no such thing as death. This state is merely a change of
dimensions, a peaceful transition.[10]

Occultists refer to death as being a transportation into another dimension. They even use this coded phrase to publicly discuss their plans to murder Christians with people being none the wiser. Here is more documentation of the actual plans to "transport into another dimension" all Christians will who not accept retraining to follow Satan right into his New Global Order:

"Guiding Spirits" of the New World Order leaders have begun to
tell them to be prepared for a simultaneous, world-wide disappear-
ance of millions of people. These spirits ascribe this phenomenon to
the fact that these people will never be able to accept Maitreya the
Christ. Their continued existence on this plane will inhibit the full
implementation of the New World Order; therefore, the Masters of
the Illuminati has made the decision to transport them into another
dimension, where their spirits will be retrained to accept the New
World Order.[11]

The New World Order threatens violence and extermination of
anyone who will not cooperate with Maitreya. David Spangler, in his
book, *Revelation: The Birth of a New Age,* stated that those who will
not cooperate will be sent to "another level of Earth's own consciousness where they can be contained and ministered to until such time
as they can be released safely into physical embodiment again."
Obviously, to be released back into physical embodiment again
means that these people must be first separated from their present
physical embodiment. The only way to accomplish this separation is
to physically kill those who cannot accept Maitreya.[12]

Jacques Cousteau stated this goal in less veiled terms:

> "The United Nation's goal is to reduce population selectively by encouraging abortion, forced sterilization, and control human reproduction, and regards two-thirds of the human population as excess baggage, with 350,000 people to be eliminated per day."[13]

The "disappearances" has been planned for a long time by the "spiritual hierarchy" who are actually spirits (demons) who communicate Satan's plans to the highest-level occultists who are even now in the process of implementing the New Age, One World Order agenda:

> The Plan is a formulation of goals and directions by the Hierarchy in respect to the Purpose given to our planet earth.[14]

Disappearances and Incarnation: God's Dramatic Invasion of Human Life?

The authors used bizarre wording to describe the disappearances and the incarnation of Jesus Christ:

> "It was a challenge to the convinced, to those who had been persuaded by God's most dramatic invasion of human life since the incarnation of Jesus Christ as a mortal baby." (*Tribulation Force,* p. 60)

The disappearances, which the writers had Bruce Barnes attribute to being the work of God, and the incarnation, which was God becoming man and coming to earth as a baby, were *invasions* of human life? An invasion is an intrusion or encroachment into a territory to conquer. The word "invasion" is a word that has an aggressive connotation.

Why would the authors want the reader to think of the incarnation of Jesus Christ in such a negative way? Satan and his followers are the only ones who consider God's coming to earth as a man as an invasion. It was an invasion of Satan's sphere of authority (the world and the souls of men) for the purpose of rescuing people from the power of darkness and delivering them into the kingdom of God's dear Son.

Jesus was manifested to destroy the works of the devil (see 1 John 3:8). That is why Satan and his followers consider Jesus' incarnation an invasion. When Jesus walked the earth healing and casting out demons, the demons certainly felt His presence was an invasion because they cried out saying:

> "What have we to do with thee, Jesus, thou Son of God? Art thou come hither to torment us before the time?" (Matt. 8:29)

No real Christian would call the incarnation of Jesus Christ an invasion. The Jews waited for this event for centuries. If Jesus did not leave heaven and come to earth to be born of a virgin, mankind would not have had the opportunity to be reconciled to God. It is positively against everything that is truly Christian to depict the incarnation of Jesus Christ as an invasion!

The authors also put the disappearances into the category of being God's "dramatic invasion of human life." Why would the authors call what they put forth as the rapture of the church by Jesus Christ an invasion? Disappearances equals invasion?

> It was a challenge to the convinced, to those who had been persuaded by God's most dramatic invasion of human life since the incarnation of Jesus Christ as a mortal baby. (*Tribulation Force*, p. 60)

The statement above is not sending the message that disappearances equal the rapture. Why the inconsistency? Why did the authors depict the disappearances in such a foreboding manner?

Media Coverage is More Evidence of the Rapture?

"If you see it on the news then it has to be true." People are conditioned to think this way, and of course the *Left Behind* characters believe that as well. Even while Rayford was still at the airport, he was already seeing televised footage of people being interviewed about the disappearances:

> Dozens of stories everywhere included eyewitnesses who had seen loved ones and friends disappear before their eyes. (*Left Behind*, p. 46)

Here is another example of news coverage of the disappearances:

> CNN showed via satellite the video of a groom disappearing while slipping the ring onto his bride's finger. (*Left Behind*, p. 47)

The reader is being led to believe that if he hears reports about mass disappearances on the news, he will know for certain the church was raptured. It is a snare for the reader to be conditioned this way because there is a logical reason other than the rapture for footage of this nature to be broadcast across the world.

Especially disturbing is the manner in which the writers had the media run footage of a funeral service where even the corpse disappeared. They even depicted a scenario where morgues reported corpse disappearances. Scripture teaches of a first resurrection, not a two-staged first resurrection to go along with a two-staged Second Coming of Jesus Christ.

Buck also watched CNN and he saw video images of disappearances caught on home videotape.

> Nothing could have been scripted like this, Buck thought, blinking slowly. (*Left Behind*, p. 110)

Oh, really? Shortly we will look at the technology that is already in place that can alter even live television coverage to make things *appear* to disappear even if this did not actually happen.

Characters Don't Just Watch the News: They Watch CNN

CNN is repeatedly mentioned in the *Left Behind* series as being *the* particular network the characters watched for all news. It is troubling that readers are being directed to trust televised mainstream news during the tribulation. News stations will be required to obey directives from their superiors (One World Order leaders) in reporting to the public. CNN founder and Time Warner vice chairman Ted Turner is committed to the goals of the United Nations:

> I've always been a strong U.N. proponent... Who was that guy who had the round table? Arthur? One for all, all for one.[15]

The *Left Behind* characters believed the news reports from CNN, the very network that was founded by those on record as being committed to bringing in the New World Order. They did not even question the news reports, which they should have done. The Bible says Christians must be as wise as serpents, and harmless as doves (Matt. 10:16). God's people will not be as wise as serpents if they believe the news fed to the masses to condition them into merging with the New World Order.

Christians are commanded to be different from the world. They must be transformed by the renewing of their minds so they can "prove what is that good, and acceptable, and perfect, will of God" (see Rom. 12:2). They must sincerely seek God so they can prove the truth worthiness of news reports, especially during times of turmoil.

Mass Disappearances Could Not Be Scripted or Staged?

Whatever we see on television should be enough to convince anybody, right? The reader is led to believe that if he sees televised "evidence" on CNN that millions of people have simultaneously disappeared, he can be certain the rapture has occurred:

> Buck couldn't take his eyes, heavy as they were, off the screen as image after image showed disappearances caught on home videotape. From some countries came professional tapes of live television shows in progress, a host's microphone landing atop his empty clothes, bouncing off his shoes, and making a racket as it rolled across the floor.
> Nothing could have been scripted like this, Buck thought, blinking slowly. (*Left Behind*, p. 110)

Yes, it could have. The following excerpt reveals how easily it could have been scripted:

> Can leading-edge modern technology insert people into a picture, and more importantly, can it make them disappear so quickly the eye can hardly see the actual disappearance? Let us return to our feature articles about technologically making people seemingly disappear:
> Deleting people or objects from live video, or inserting pre-recorded people or objects into *live scenes*, is only the beginning of the deceptions becoming possible." There we have the nub of the problem solved; once you understand the science behind this new technique of unprecedented deception, you will come right back to this statement:
> There you have the stark facts; MIT's Technology Magazine is telling us that people can be removed or inserted into live scenes. This means that a scene being recorded "LIVE" can have people artificially deleted [removed] or inserted, with no one being the wiser.
> In NEWS1375, referenced above, we postulated that one of the techniques the Illuminati would use to convince Christians that they had been left behind in a Rapture would be a prerecorded short movie in which the entire scenario were shot as if it were a live newscast. TV movies have been produced and aired on this premise just a few years ago, and were so effective that a disclaimer came on the screen at the beginning and end of the show, and after each commercial, telling the viewer that the action being depicted was not a real live newscast; that is how effective these shows were"[16]

The technology to stage a fake rapture does exist. Seeing images of people disappearing on television is not proof the rapture of the church has occurred.

Death Euphemisms Associated with Disappearances

Rayford grieved over the loss of his wife:

> At first, becoming attuned to his emotions had been revelatory. It had allowed him to care deeply for his daughter, to really grieve over the loss of his wife and son, and to understand how much he had loved them. (*The Indwelling*, p. 70)

> Rayford Steele could not sleep. For some reason he was overcome anew with grief and remorse over the loss of his wife and son. (*Left Behind*, p. 298)

Rayford was filled with grief and remorse over the *loss* of his wife and son. Why should he be filled with grief? His wife and son were supposedly raptured and in glory with the Lord. If their disappearances really evidenced they went to heaven, he would be relieved they were in the arms of in the arms of the Lord rather than living during the tribulation.

During Bruce Barnes' memorial service, Rayford used some strange-sounding words in referring to the departure of Bruce's wife and children from this earth:

> He proceeded to tell when and where Bruce was born and when and where he died. "He was preceded by his wife, a daughter, and two sons, who were raptured by the church." (*Nicolae*, p. 311)

Precede means "to go before" in this context. In all funerals, the people who "preceded" the deceased were people who died previously. This is a *strange context* in which to put people who were supposedly translated to heaven. If Bruce's wife and children did not die, then why was it presented this way initially, and then "fixed" by the addition of a phrase that indicated they were raptured?

> Bruce had pleaded with Rayford and Chloe to hear his own testimony of losing his wife and three young children in the middle of the night. (*Nicolae*, p. 313)

Why were the people who supposedly went to heaven in the rapture described as being *lost* by their relatives who remained on the earth? Why were the people who were "left behind" never happy for those who were supposed to be in heaven? I find it odd that there was no rejoicing that their loved ones were safe in heaven with Jesus, and no discussions among the "left behind" about their glorious new home. Instead, the characters were *grieving* over them. This is more consistent with the enactment of The Plan and the snatching of believers from their homes in the middle of the night than of Jesus translating His saints into glory.

In the following excerpt, the people who did not disappear or die were called survivors:

> Worldwide chaos ensued. Planes, trains, buses, and cars crashed, ships sank, homes burned, grieving survivors committed suicide. (*Tribulation Force*, p. vii)

Why would not going to heaven be something that a person survives?

If Christians Will Be Raptured Before the Tribulation, Why is this Statement on the *Left Behind* Website?

If the people at *Leftbehind.com* believe Christians will be removed from the earth in a pre-tribulation rapture, why is this statement, which is directed to Christians, in the "Discussion Guide For the Mark"?

> In his teaching (see chapter 9), Tsion tells his readers that if they refuse the mark of the beast, they will be beheaded. He goes on to say that we worry whether at that hour we will be found lacking courage, loyalty, and faithfulness. Then he reassures his readers that the God who calls them to the ultimate sacrifice will also give them the power to endure it. How do you feel when you think about getting killed in this way as a martyr? Do you look to your own resources of courage and loyalty, or do you look to God to supply what you will need in that hour?[17]

The writer of the "Mark" discussion guide asked the reader, "How do you feel when you think about getting killed in this way as a martyr?" and "or do you look to God to supply what you need in that hour?" This does not sound like the writer really believes that Christians will escape the tribulation and the mark of the beast via a pre-tribulation rapture.

Comparison Between Numbers Killed and Numbers Disappeared

> He turned CNN on low so it wouldn't interrupt his sleep, and he watched the world roundup before dozing off. (*Left Behind*, p. 109)
>
> Images from around the globe were almost more than he could take, but news was his business. He remembered the many earthquakes and wars of the last decade and the nightly coverage that was so moving. Now here was a thousand times more of the same, all on the same day. Never in history had he seen more people killed in one day than those who disappeared all at once. Had they been killed? Were they dead? Would they be back? (*Left Behind*, pp. 109-10)

It is ominous that the authors had Buck think about the number of people known to be killed in one day and the number of people who disappeared all at once. This is actually part of The Plan:

> "The Plan" which includes a "cleansing action" [author's note: the murder of millions] that must take place to remove negative and evil elements from the world before the New Age of peace can be fully ushered in. [8]

God is Behind the Population Decimation?

The writers inserted into *The Indwelling* a very disturbing sentence that does not go along with the flow of the surrounding text at all. It is a print subliminal:

> Tsion taught that part of the population decimation might be God's way of removing his most incorrigible enemies in anticipation of the coming epic. (*The Indwelling*, p. 36)

The population decimation during the time of the tribulation will be Satan's doing. It will be his brief time to be openly worshipped as God on a global scale. His followers will destroy huge numbers of people, including non-Christians, who do not directly fit into furthering The Plan.

In fact, it is the specific plan of the Coming One (one title of the New Age Christ) to destroy life:

> In "The Great Invocation," a "prayer" highly reverenced among New Agers and chanted to "invoke" the Maitreya, says, "Let Light an Love and Power and Death, Fulfill the purposes of the Coming One.[19]

Christians must not despair and give in to fear simply because these are the enemy's *plans*. God is able to do "exceeding abundantly above all that we ask or think, according to the power that worketh in us" (see Eph. 3:20). He will receive glory in the church by Jesus Christ even during the tribulation, and one of the ways He will do this is by protecting His overcoming church from being overcome by the beast during the time ahead. The Plan is to kill all Christians, Jews, and other dissidents, but that does not mean this will happen. If the church will repent and return to the Lord Jesus Christ in single-eyed obedience, He will order her steps during the tribulation.

Material Things Left Behind is Proof Positive the Rapture Has Occurred?

Pastor Billings preached on his videotaped sermon,

> "I believe that all such people were literally taken from the earth, leaving everything material behind. If you have discovered that millions of people are missing and that babies and children have vanished, you know what I'm saying is true." (*Left Behind*, p. 211)

We have from this authoritative source that we can know for sure the rapture has taken place if:

1. Millions of people are missing, and

2. Babies and children have vanished

The pastor even said that this was the fulfillment of the promise of Christ when He said, "I will come again and receive you unto myself; that where I am, there you may be also." The Bible does not teach us that personal effects left behind by missing people are signs that the Lord Jesus Christ has come and taken His church. In fact, the Bible teaches about the signs that will come *before* His coming, not after.

> The sun shall be turned into darkness, and the moon into blood, before the great and notable day of the Lord come. (Acts 2:20)
>
> Immediately after the tribulation of those days shall the sun be darkened, and the moon shall not give her light, and the stars shall fall from heaven, and the powers of the heavens shall be shaken: And then shall appear the sign of the Son of man in heaven: and then shall all the tribes of the earth mourn, and they shall see the Son of man coming in the clouds of heaven with power and great glory. (Matt. 24:29-30)

The sign of the Son of man is what Jesus said it would be. Saying that it is clothing left behind and massive disappearances is adding to the Word of God.

The Bible does not teach a two-staged rapture, but the *Left Behind* series teaches that if certain things happen *that can be staged* then the rapture of the church has definitely taken place. The real return of the Lord Jesus Christ for His bride will be impossible to be staged.

Bruce related the evidences that convinced him the rapture had taken place:

> "When the baby was not in his crib, I turned the light on, stuck my head out the door and called down the hall for my wife. No answer. Then I noticed the baby's footie pajamas in the crib, and I knew." (*Left Behind,* p. 193)
>
> "No trace of her, 'cept her clothes, and you know what that means."
> "She's gone?" (*Left Behind,* p. 106)

Missing persons and clothing that is removed and left behind is not proof that the rapture has occurred. The only proof the Christian can safely believe is what is recorded in the Holy Bible about what Jesus actually *said* about His return for His church. (see Matt.24) This must be read, believed, and clung to; no one else's words can be trusted.

Real Christians Disappear; False Christians Left Behind?

The following excerpt reveals Rayford's thoughts as he looked through his house for his wife, Irene:

> "Was it possible she had gone somewhere? Visited someone? Left him a message? But if he did find her, what would that say about her own faith? Would that prove this was not the Rapture she believed in? Or would it mean she was lost, just like he was? For her sake, if this was the Rapture, he hoped she *was* gone." (*Left Behind*, p. 67)

This is one of the most disturbing passages contained in the "disappearances" theme. The authors had Rayford think that since mass disappearances have occurred, if Irene was not gone, then she was not truly saved. The Christian reader is being led to think that if he hears about widespread vanishings and he has not been taken, then he is to automatically think he is a phony Christian.

> I've got relatives who believe the space alien stuff. I've got an uncle who thinks it was Jesus, but he also thinks Jesus forgot *him*." (*Left Behind*, p. 355) [emphasis in the original]

Remember that Satan's followers want to overthrow the faith of as many Christians as possible so they can easily bring in their long-awaited One World Government. The tribulation period is the final phase of history before the Second Coming of Jesus Christ. God will give the world a full measure of the god it already runs after. Satan's most sought after plan is to get Christians to abandon their faith in God and to replace it with trust in him. He will use any deception they will accept in order to accomplish this.

It is The Plan to cause Christians worldwide to disappear, seemingly simultaneously. If the Christians who did not disappear become distraught because they thought Jesus forgot them, they are playing right into Satan's hands.

For your very soul's sake you must reject the lie that "not disappeared" equals not being truly saved. Jesus promised to return for those who love His appearing, and He will not fail – period. If you are a follower of the Lord Jesus Christ, a disciple indeed, as Jesus calls those who continue in His Word, you will be able to count on every promise Jesus made to you in the Bible. Please do not allow situations that can be manipulated by people (such as televised broadcasts, radio broadcasts, and other forms of media) to affect what you believe about the Lord Jesus Christ. The scripture cannot be broken, and Jesus has never, and will never, break His own Word. He will return when He said He would – immediately after the tribulation – in the clouds with great glory.

7

THE BIBLE ON THE MARK OF THE BEAST

All scripture is given by the inspiration of God (see 2 Tim. 3:16). We can live physically with mere physical sustenance, but our spiritual lives are dependent upon *every* word in the precious Bible.

> "It is written, Man shall not live by bread alone, but by every word that proceedeth out of the mouth of God." (Matt. 4:4)

The Holy Bible, which is the written Word of God, is forever true and changeless, without error, and pure. It is literally our "measuring line for truth."[1] The Word of God is absolute truth, which means that it is unquestionably true without exception. Absolute truth is the opposite of relativism, which is a doctrine that denies the existence of absolutes. The scriptures are profitable for doctrine, reproof, and instruction in righteousness. The scriptures are very precious, and whoever despises the Word shall be destroyed (Ps. 19:10, Prov. 13:13).

Taking the absolute truth of God's Word and trying to make people think that any part of it is relative is an example of despising God's Word. This is what the authors did with the mark of the beast doctrine in *The Mark* and in *Desecration*. They devised a subplot in which a Christian character unwillingly received the mark of the beast and did not lose his salvation – he was represented as being exempt from drinking of the wine of the wrath of God – as promised in the unchangeable Word of God.

Before we look at how the authors used the storyline to manipulate the reader into thinking that a Christian in certain circumstances can have the mark of the beast and still be in God's family, let us look briefly at the "mark of the beast" doctrine as revealed in the Holy Bible.

What is the Mark of the Beast?

> And he causeth all, both small and great, rich and poor, free and bond, to receive a mark in their right hand, or in their foreheads:
> And that no man might buy or sell, save he that had the mark, or the name of the beast, or the number of his name.
> Here is wisdom. Let him that hath understanding count the number of the beast: for it is the number of a man; and his number is Six hundred threescore and six. (Rev. 13:16-18)

The mark is something the beast (Satan's world ruler during the time of the tribulation) will cause everyone in the world to receive in their right hand or forehead. No one will be allowed to participate in the world's economy without having the mark, the name, or the number of the beast:

> And the third angel followed them, saying with a loud voice, If any man shall worship the beast and his image, and receive his mark in his forehead, or in his hand,
> The same shall drink of the wine of the wrath of God, which is poured out without mixture into the cup of his indignation; and he shall be tormented with fire and brimstone in the presence of the holy angels, and in the presence of the Lamb:
> And the smoke of their torment ascendeth up forever and ever: and they have no rest day nor night, who worship the beast and his image, and whosoever receiveth the mark of his name. (Rev. 14:9-11)

If any man shall worship the beast and his image, and receive his mark in his forehead or in his hand, he shall "drink of the wine of the wrath of God" which means he shall be tormented with fire and brimstone. This is a sin for which there is no repentance and no forgiveness. Anyone who receives the mark of the beast and worships the beast and his image will reap eternal damnation.

Caused, Not Forced, to Take the Mark

There is a *big difference* in meaning between the word "caused" or "causeth" (King James Bible) and "forced" (NIV) and it is such a big difference that doctrine is actually changed.

"Cause" means "to bring into existence or effect by agency, power or influence." The King James Bible says, "And he *causeth* all, both small and great, rich and poor, free and bond, to receive a mark in their right hand, or in their foreheads" (Rev. 13:16).

"Force" means "to compel or constrain to do by the exertion of a power not resistible." The NIV says, "He also forced everyone, small and great, rich and poor, free and slave, to receive a mark on his right hand or on his forehead" (Rev. 13:16).

Since "caused" and "forced" have different definitions, both words are not correct. Laws cause people to do things, but they do not *physically* force them. People who disobey the law receive a penalty. It may even be beheading, but it is still a penalty. That is why they are caused to obey. They want to avoid the penalty. They make the choice to comply with the law, avoid the law by fleeing before the law is enacted or before they are caught, or to accept the penalty.

"Forcing" people to comply by overtaking them with an irresistible power removes the power of choice from them. A person who is forced to do something is not responsible because someone else is imposing their will on him. Everyone who is forced to take the mark would automatically be in compliance with the stated law because no one would be able to choose to disobey. There would be no need for a penalty if there were no choice but to obey.

Remember, the severity of the penalty is not what defines force. Satan would love to have the ability to force Christians to worship him and take his identifying mark, but he is unable to do this. That is why he hopes he will be able to *deceive* them into not holding fast the beginning of their confidence steadfast until the end so they would spiritually faint and confess Antichrist and take his mark. He can accomplish this only if they give heed to seducing spirits through false prophets that tell them they will be forgiven if they do this.

God will not send people to an eternity of smoke and torment in the Lake of Fire because someone else physically forced them to commit this unpardonable, irreversible, unforgivable sin. The Bible warns that

> ...If any man worship the beast and his image, and receive his mark in his forehead, or in his hand,

> the same shall drink of the wine of the wrath of God… and he shall be tormented with fire and brimstone in the presence of the holy angels, and in the presence of the Lamb. (Rev. 14:9-10)

The teaching that a Christian can be "forced" to take the mark of the beast and be forgiven for it is the most dangerous doctrine to assail the church in recent history. It is a denial of the straightforward Bible doctrine that those who receive the mark of the beast are doomed to smoke and torment forever. This false doctrine, taught in *The Mark* and *Desecration*, actually makes provision for this unforgivable sin under the false, unbiblical condition of being physically forced.

You must rebuke and renounce this doctrine of devils immediately. Cast down this imagination that is exalting itself against the knowledge of God and seeking to conform your thoughts to the image of Satan.

Patient Saints Will Get Victory Over the Mark

The Bible describes the fate of those who do not get victory over the mark of the beast and the worship of the beast and his image:

> And the smoke of their torment ascendeth up for ever and ever: and they have no rest day nor night, who worship the beast and his image, and whosoever receiveth the mark of his name. (Rev. 14:11)

Praise God, the very next verse tells how we may get victory over the mark:

> Here is the patience of the saints: here are they that keep the commandments of God, and the faith of Jesus. (Rev. 14:12)

Patient saints – those who *keep* the commandments of God and the faith of Jesus – are the Christians who will get victory over the mark. It is in patience that we will continue to possess our souls, both now and in the tribulation (see Luke 21:19). Those who get victory over the mark are those saints who truly bow to the Lord

Jesus Christ as King over all the kingdoms of the world right now, and will continue to do this during the time Antichrist.

> And I saw as it were a sea of glass mingled with fire: and them that had gotten the victory over the beast, and over his image, and over his mark, and over the number of his name, stand on the sea of glass, having the harps of God.
> And they sing the song of Moses the servant of God, and the song of the Lamb, saying, Great and marvelous are thy works, Lord God Almighty; just and true are thy ways, thou King of Saints. (Rev. 15:2-3)

Single-Eyed Saints Will Get Victory Over the Mark

Those who keep the commandments of God have the faith of Jesus, while those who keep the commandments of the beast have the faith of Satan. In that evil day, Christians will have to choose whom they will serve just like they choose whom they will serve in this present time. When the mark of the beast becomes the law of the land, any Christian who has not been overcoming all along will be overcome. Christians who presently conform to this world because they refuse to deny themselves and resist its deceptive allure will not suddenly stop loving this world and return to their First Love when darkness overtakes the earth. Those who willfully walk in spiritual darkness now will not be alarmed by it later. They will not even recognize it if they are already having fellowship with darkness in the form of compromise. Jesus said that if we walk in darkness we will not know where we are going (see John 12:35).

This is the reason Christians must keep the commandments of Jesus and "walk in the light as He is in the light" (1 John 1:7) and obediently "walk as children of light" (Eph. 5:8). "Ye are all the children of light, and the children of the day: we are not of the night, nor of darkness." (1 Thess. 5:5).

Jesus said,

> The light of the body is the eye: therefore when thine eye is single, thy whole body also is full of light; but when thine eye is evil, thy body also is full of darkness.

Take heed therefore that the light which is in thee be not darkness. (Luke 11:34-35)

The light in a Christian *can* become darkness, and Jesus said we must take heed the spiritual light in us does not become darkness. When a Christian is single-hearted in obeying the light God has given him, he has a single eye, and his whole body is full of spiritual light. He is walking in the light just like Jesus walked in the light (see 1 John 1:7). In this blessed state, he is not allowing any spiritual darkness into his life, just like there is no darkness in Jesus' life.

But when a Christian has an eye that is evil, it means he is not single-hearted in obedience to the light given him by the Word of God, which is a lamp unto his feet and a light unto his path. A Christian does not have to be disobeying the Word of Christ in all things to have an evil eye. If he is holding back obedience to God in any area of his life, he is guilty of having an evil eye.

Jesus said, "I am come a light into the world, that whosoever believeth on me should not abide in darkness." Abide means "to live." If a Christian lives in partial darkness (the part he enjoys) and does not wholeheartedly and unreservedly obey God, he has an evil eye and his whole body will become full of spiritual darkness if he does not repent. This is how the spiritual light that is in a Christian *can* be turned into spiritual darkness (see Luke 11:35).

Sadly, this is the state of most Christians today, as the falling away of the church is picking up speed. They do not have single eyes, and they think that God is satisfied with some of their heart's devotion while they keep back the rest of their heart for themselves. If Christians continue in this state of being lukewarm, they will be *deceived just like the rest of the world* into receiving the mark of the beast when it becomes mandated. The Bible knowledge they have about the mark of the beast will not protect them because God Himself will send His delusion upon them so they will believe the lie. They will have brought this judgment upon themselves because they believed not the truth, but instead, had pleasure in unrighteousness. (See 2 Thess. 1-12)

Christians Who Become "Offended in Christ" Will Not Get Victory Over the Beast and His Mark

The opposite of having the patience of the saints is becoming offended in Christ. This will be the state of Christians who do not expect to be here during the time of the tribulation. Jesus said He would return in the clouds of heaven in power and great glory immediately after the tribulation, He prayed that we would *not* be taken out of the world during tribulation, but that we be kept from the evil. In spite of His clear promises, many will become offended in Him (see Matt. 24:28-30, John 17:15).

Christians who have great faith in their teachers' promises rather than Jesus' plainly spoken words, will feel betrayed when the tribulation begins and they have not been taken out of the world. The promises of our Lord Jesus Christ concerning when He would return are recorded in scripture:

> Immediately after the tribulation of those days shall the sun be darkened, and the moon shall not give her light, and the stars shall fall from heaven, and the powers of the heavens shall be shaken:
> And then shall appear the sign of the Son of man in heaven: and then shall all the tribes of the earth mourn, and they shall see the Son of man coming in the clouds of heaven with power and great glory. (Matt. 24:29-30)

If we find verses that we have been told have a meaning that contradicts the words of our Lord, whose name is Truth, we must believe His words and not believe any interpretations of verses that contradict His very words. Any doctrine that is *against* the words of the Lord Jesus Christ is antichrist. When speaking the truth, if the person omits something that is necessary to know, then he is lying. Omitting parts of the truth so the hearer does not receive the full message is the same thing as lying. Jesus Christ said He would return immediately after the tribulation of those days. He so very kindly said these days would be shortened for the sake of the elect (see Mark 13:20). If He were going to return another time (before the tribulation) for the elect of God, He would have said so. Jesus Christ does not mislead His people by saying one thing and *meaning* another. (Satan does this to his followers, but the Lord Jesus Christ does not.) One of Jesus' names is Truth. He is the Way, the Truth, and the Life.

Many Christians have read commentaries and study Bibles and think it is too simplistic to take Jesus at His word and believe that He will return when He *stated* that He would return. For those who still believe this way, please remember Jesus' words, and do not become offended in Him, no matter what happens.

Any Christian can become so offended in Christ that he falls away from the faith. We must purpose to guard our hearts and continue to be rooted and built up in Him, and established in the faith. We must beware of any men who would spoil our faith through philosophy and vain deceit, after the tradition of men and after the rudiments of the world, and not after Christ's very own words (see Col. 2:8).

John the Baptist Wondered if He Should Look For Another

John the Baptist, the prophet of God who prepared the way of the Lord and baptized Jesus was almost at the point of becoming offended in the Lord Jesus Christ during a time of great suffering in his life. Indeed, while he was languishing in Herod's prison, he sent two of his disciples to Jesus to ask these questions:

> "Art he that should come? Or look we look for another?"
> (Luke 7:19)

Why would this single-eyed prophet of God be on the verge of becoming offended in Jesus Christ, even to the point that he thought he might not even be the real Christ? We know the Pharisees were certainly offended in Jesus because he could see right through their soul-subverting hypocrisies.

John the Baptist was imprisoned because he spoke the Word of God to Herod regarding his brother's wife, Herodias: "It is not lawful for thee to have her" (Matt. 14:4). John the Baptist was godly, and yes, he suffered persecution for it.

Why did Jesus allow this to happen? Even this faithful prophet of God, who was Jesus' cousin and had known Him all his life, had second thoughts about the true identity of his Lord because of the severe persecution he was undergoing. If John could be almost offended in Christ and question if he should look for another, how much more could we if we do not understand that just as John suffered for his faith, *all* that live godly in Christ Jesus will also suffer persecution. We *must* heed Jesus' words:

> "And blessed is he, whosoever shall not be offended in me."
> (Luke 7:23)

The Mark of the Beast and Worship of the Beast Go Together

The authors of the *Left Behind* series *separated* the soul-damning acts of being marked with the beast and worshipping the beast in order to try and justify the fact that Chang remained a Christian after he received the mark of the beast. Chang had the mark of the beast, but the character Tsion said he did not *accept* this mark, and that he would not worship him:

> "You did not *accept* the mark of Antichrist, nor will you worship him." (*Desecration,* p. 10) [emphasis in the original]

In the Bible, the mark of the beast and worshipping the beast *go together*:

> And the third angel followed them, saying with a loud voice, If any man *worship the beast and his image*, and *receive his mark* in his forehead, or in his hand, (Rev. 14:9)

> And the smoke of their torment ascendeth up for ever and ever: and they have no rest day nor night, who *worship the beast and his image*, and whosoever *receiveth the mark* of his name. (Rev. 14:11)

> And the first went, and poured out his vial upon the earth; and there fell a noisome and grievous sore upon the men which had the *mark of the beast,* and upon them which *worshipped his image.* (Rev. 16:2)

> And the beast was taken, and with him the false prophet that wrought miracles before him, with which he deceived them that had received the *mark of the beast*, and them that *worshipped his image*. These both were cast alive into a lake of fire burning with brimstone. (Rev. 19:20)

It is unconscionable to present the teaching that you can have the mark of allegiance to Antichrist (the beast) as long as you do not take the mark with a willing heart, and as long as you do not worship him. It is plain in scripture that these two acts go together, and in fact, taking the mark *is* an act of worship to the beast.

Even Satan knows that obedience equals worship. It is tragic that his false teachers have deceived Christians into believing that the Lord Jesus Christ does not *require* obedience from His followers. Satan is a counterfeiter. Whom do you think the devil counterfeits by requiring his disciples to obey him? He counterfeits the Lord Jesus Christ, who is the "author of eternal salvation unto all them that *obey* Him" (Heb. 5:9).

Comply or Die

Christians who have been walking with Jesus with single-eyed obedience *before* the tribulation begins will have their bodies full of spiritual light, and they will able to spiritually discern the mark of the beast and the worship of the beast for what it is: the worship of Satan. The children of God will reject this spiritual darkness outright because the light that is in them will expose it for what it really is.

These children of God will be living during a time when they will be betrayed by parents, brethren, kinfolk, and friends. Some of them will die because of this betrayal into the hands of the authorities. These saints of God, who have been living godly in Christ Jesus all along and have as a result suffered some persecution, will be hated by all nations for Jesus' sake.

This will occur because almost everyone will be thoroughly conditioned to think that anyone who does not take the mark and go along with the New World Order is against the better global order, and is an enemy. Because these people have been serving sin all along, they will have darkened minds and actually think they are serving God by delivering up Christians to their death. This is the form of government the beast will bring in. That is why Jesus said that "many will be offended, and shall betray one another, and shall hate one another" (see Luke 21:12-19, Matt. 24: 9-13).

It will definitely be a time when choosing whom you will serve will be everybody's business. People will be rewarded for turning in all dissenters for the punishment they will have been brainwashed into thinking is the proper penalty for those who oppose the beast.

Christians who did not flee, or who were turned in to the authorities, will have to face the guillotine or worse:

> And I saw thrones, and they sat upon them, and judgment was given unto them: and I saw the souls of them that were beheaded for the witness of Jesus, and for the word of God, and which had not worshipped the beast, neither his image, neither had received his mark upon their foreheads, or in their hands; and they lived and reigned with Christ a thousand years. (Rev. 20:4)

The worldly, and therefore already overcome Christian, will *not* get victory over the mark. His darkened mind will rationalize away the Biblical penalty of taking the mark. He will be deceived into taking the mark the same way he had been deceived into yielding himself to serve sin before the tribulation even began (see Rom. 6:15-18).

Only the Christian who has been denying himself, taking up his cross, and following Jesus *all along* will be able to overcome the beast and get victory over the mark. This saint, who has been walking in the Spirit and keeping the works of Jesus all along, will continue to overcome when the world is overtaken by Antichrist's regime, which is all-out satanism. This is the only kind of Christian who will overcome him by the blood of the Lamb, and by the word of his testimony, and by not loving his life unto the death (see Rev. 12:11).

The beloved saints of God will overcome Satan during the tribulation the *same way* they overcome him today. They will not be able to live sinful lives like the characters of the *Left Behind* series and then suddenly have dying grace that literally renders them *unable* to commit the sin of taking the mark of the beast. The *Left Behind* series actually teaches this to the reader through Tsion Ben-Judah (the main spiritual authority figure in the series) and it literally sets up the reader to be spiritually destroyed. There will be no "line up and decide" scenario when the mark becomes required by law. This decision to die daily and take up our cross and follow Jesus must be made long before the mark is required.

The grace to not be overcome and take the mark of the beast will reign during the tribulation the same way grace reigns in the life of a true Christian right now: through righteousness. Grace does not reign through unrighteousness, as the *Left Behind* series teaches. Grace will *not* abound toward the Christian when it is time to get victory over the mark if he has been serving unrighteousness all along. God forbid that Christians continue in sin and think they will have the grace to get victory over the mark of the beast. If they continue to love their own lives today, they will *not* suddenly die to themselves and not love their own lives unto death during the tribulation (see Rom. 6:1-2).

In the next chapter, you will see how the *Left Behind* series presents many false teachings about the mark of the beast. They are teachings which, if not exposed as being the doctrines of Satan rather than the doctrines of the Bible, will result in the eternal damnation of many people.

8

BY THEIR MARKS YE SHALL KNOW THEM?

Satan's agents will use any idea from any source, including teachings from purportedly Christian fiction novels about the last days, to destroy the people of God.

The "mark of the believer" deception, repeated many times in the *Left Behind* series, is one such teaching they can and will use against Christians during the tribulation *if* they can get away with it. In this chapter you will discover the lengths to which the authors went in order to get across to the reader that the teaching of a visible "mark of the believer" is actually taught in the scriptures, and that Christians can really know each other by their "marks" during the tribulation.

The authors used the propaganda technique of repetition to thoroughly embed into the reader's mind the false teaching that during the tribulation, those who *really* belong to Jesus Christ will have a visible mark on their foreheads that can be seen only by other Christians. They want the reader to believe that a Christian will not be able to see his own "mark" but that he will know he is truly in the family of God because others with a visible mark will tell him they see *his* "mark." Only other Christians, *not* Antichrist's followers, will be able to see this mark. This is one of the most dangerous false teachings in the *Left Behind* series. If the reader believes the "mark of the believer" teaching is a real Bible doctrine, he will be spiritually destroyed.

Warming Up the Reader Up for the "Christian Mark"

In every single instance where the authors presented a false teaching that is blatantly against scripture, they used a slow and furtive approach in presenting the "new and untrue" doctrine to the reader. They always presented new doctrines in incremental stages so the reader would slowly warm up to receive the teachings rather than reject them out of hand.

The earliest warming up for the "mark of the believer" doctrine was when Rayford was beginning to witness to Mac. He was filled with fear because he had no idea whether Mac was sincerely interested in hearing about Christ or merely pretending to be interested so he could betray him later.

The authors used prayer as the foundation to present this new teaching. Because the new doctrine was presented as coming from God in answer to prayer, its credibility was greatly enhanced in the mind of the reader:

> Rayford covered his eyes briefly. "God," he prayed silently, "all I can do is trust you and follow my instincts. I believe this man is sincere. If he's not, keep me from saying anything I shouldn't. If he is sincere, I don't want to keep from telling him what he needs to know. You've been so overt, so clear with Buck and Tsion. Couldn't you give me a sign? Anything that would assure me I'm doing the right thing?" (*Soul Harvest*. p. 46)

The "right thing" that Rayford needed to be sure about, was that he needed to know who was a real Christian and who was not. He needed to know for sure so he would not end up losing his life for Jesus' sake. The reader understandably empathizes with Rayford's fear of trusting the wrong person because he knows it will be literally against the law to be a Christian during the tribulation. This is how the writers set the reader up to accept a visible mark upon a Christian.

Rayford Prays Again for a Sign to See Whether Mac Was Sincere

Much of *Soul Harvest* is devoted to Rayford's fearful and reluctant witnessing to Mac. He worried himself sick that he might actually have to pay a price for the testimony of Jesus, and I don't think this has escaped the reader's notice. "How to be a Christian during the tribulation and not have to suffer persecution for it" is a repeating message in the *Left Behind* series. Rayford was petrified that Mac was merely leading him on, and that he was possibly a game-player ready to turn him in for witnessing. Rayford had already said so much to Mac that he knew he was in certain trouble if Mac was not sincere:

> But Rayford was already beyond the point of no return. Again he prayed silently that God might give him a sign whether Mac was sincere. If he wasn't, he was one of the better actors Rayford had seen. It was hard to trust anyone anymore. (*Soul Harvest*, p. 107)

The authors reminded the reader of Rayford's (and one day, the reader's) dilemma. He needed God to give him a foolproof way to determine whom he could trust. This is the second time the authors had this character pray for a sign.

Rayford Prays a Third Time For a Sign

The writers had Rayford, one of the main characters and hero in the *Left Behind* series, all but completely lose the testimony of Jesus by his shamefully depicted "save his own life" attitude in witnessing to Mac.

> He seemed sincere. But Rayford didn't really know him, didn't know his background. Mac could be a loyalist, a Carpathia plant. Rayford had already exposed himself to mortal danger if Mac was merely entrapping him. Silently he prayed again, "God, how will I know for sure?" (*Soul Harvest,* p. 133)

The reader has been thoroughly primed to believe that God, in answer to Rayford's prayer, will give him a sign so he will know whom he can trust, and whom he should be wary of.

God's Unbiblical "Answer": A "Cross-Shaped" Smudge

Rayford continued in his anguished uncertainty regarding Mac's conversion story. He was so worried that Mac could be merely pretending to be a Christian, that he agonized over whether he should have even witnessed to him at all. The stage is set for the writers to bring in God's "answer" to Rayford's prayer for a sign:

> "Did you shower this morning, Mac?"
> "Always. What do you mean?"
> "You've got a smudge on your forehead." (*Soul Harvest*, p 171)

Mac, no matter how hard he tried, could not see the smudge on his forehead while he stared into the mirror with Rayford by his side. Rayford described the smudge in more detail:

> "Right there! That charcoal-looking smudge about the size of a thumbprint." (*Soul Harvest*, p. 172)

Rayford continued:

> "Yes! There it is! I can see it!"
> "What?!"
> "It's a cross! Oh, my word! It's a cross, Mac!" (*Soul Harvest*, p. 172)

The story has God answering Rayford's repeated prayers by putting a visible smudge on Mac's forehead, which, upon close observation, was shaped like a cross.

When Mac looked into the mirror, he could not see the cross on his own forehead, and asked,

> "Why can't I see it?" (*Soul Harvest*, p. 172)

> Rayford leaned into the mirror and held his own hair away from his forehead. "Wait! Do I have one too? Nope, I don't see one."

> Mac paled. "You do! He said. "Let me look at that."
> Rayford could barely breathe as Mac stared. "Unbelievable!" Mac said. It *is* a cross. I can see yours and you can see mine, but we can't see our own." (*Soul Harvest*, pp. 172-73)

There will be serious repercussions for any Christian or Christian-to-be who believes this doctrinal invention. I will get to that after I show you how much effort the authors put forth to get the reader to believe this fabrication.

> "Mac," Rayford said, fighting tears, "I can hardly believe this. I prayed for a sign, and God answered. I needed a sign. How can I know who to trust these days?" (*Soul Harvest*, p. 174)

Rayford Tests Smudge on an Unbeliever

> A young assistant from the communications center said, "Excuse me, sirs, but whichever one of you is Captain Steele has a phone call."
> "Be right there," Rayford said. "By the way, have I got a smudge on my forehead right here?"
> The young man looked. "No sir. Don't think so." (*Soul Harvest*, p. 174)

The authors immediately directed the reader to think that an unbeliever cannot see God's cross-shaped smudge upon a Christian's forehead.

Smudge is Called "a Mark" For the First Time

The writers portrayed a doctor being curious about what looked like a bruise on Buck's forehead. With Buck's permission, the doctor examined Buck's hairline:

> "You *do* have a mark there," the doctor said. He pushed on it and around it. "No pain?" (*Soul Harvest*, p. 178)

The doctor innocently called what he thought was a bruise on Buck's forehead, a mark. This was the way the authors introduced the concept of calling the cross-shaped smudge a "mark." Neither the doctor nor Buck knew that "God" was now acting contrary to scripture and placing a physical "mark" upon His followers, so they had to find this out by the process of discovery:

> "You know," Buck said, "you've got something on your forehead too. Looks like a smudge." (*Soul Harvest,* p. 179)
>
> "Obviously, nobody but fellow believers can see these marks." (*Soul Harvest,* p. 183)

The authors "solved" one of the most serious concerns a Christian will have during the tribulation by devising a "Bible doctrine" that directly addresses this fear. They are literally teaching that true Christians will be invisible to the satanists in their Hour of Dark Power. This is literally leading Christians to the slaughter if they fall for this lie.

Deceiving the Reader into Thinking the Bible Teaches Christians Will Have a Visible Seal

Tsion Ben-Judah is the Bible scholar of the Tribulation Force, as well as being the spiritual leader to many Christians via the internet. The authors used this authority figure to lend credence to their revolutionary, anti-Biblical doctrines they want the reader to believe:

> Tsion seemed to stare desperately at Buck. Suddenly he said, "Yes! Cameron! We have the seal, visible to only other believers."
> "What are you talking about?"
> "The seventh chapter of Revelation tells of 'the servants of our God' being sealed on their foreheads. That has to be what this is!"
> (*Soul Harvest,* pp. 193-94)

The scripture verses in the seventh chapter of Revelation do *not* say all Christians will have a visible seal. They do not even say that *any* Christians will have a visible seal.

Before I cite the verse, I wanted you to notice how the authors taught relativism by having the characters find visible seals on their foreheads, and *then* they had the Bible scholar character cite the seventh chapter of Revelation, and then submit this portion of scripture to the character's experience. Let us look at the verses and see how the authors had Tsion cite a verse that is *not* saying what they had him say it teaches:

> And I saw another angel ascending from the east, having the seal of the living God: and he cried with a loud voice to the four angels, to whom it was given to hurt the earth and the sea,
> Saying Hurt not the earth, neither the sea, nor the trees, till we have sealed the servants of our God in their foreheads.
> And I heard the number of them which were sealed: and there were sealed an hundred and forty and four thousand of all the tribes of the children of Israel. (Rev. 7:2-4)

There are contradictions between what the *Bible* teaches about the sealing of the servants of God and what the authors want the reader to believe:

1. Rev. 7:3 says the angels will seal the servants of God in their foreheads, but *Soul Harvest* has God be the one who has done this in answer to prayer.

2. Rev. 7:4 says those that will be sealed by the angels of God will be 144,000 of all the tribes of Israel; *Soul Harvest* has *all* true Christians being sealed.

Nowhere in these verses in Revelation do we see any mention of a visible seal, or a seal that cannot be seen by the Christian on his own person, but only by other Christians. And of course there is no mention that Satan's followers would not be able to see this visible seal, thereby guaranteeing that Christians would be able to be "secret agent" followers of Christ.

The authors introduced the "mark of the believer" doctrine in a blatantly antichrist manner. They authenticated this false teaching in the story by using God (in answer to Rayford's prayers), and the Holy Bible (in Tsion's reference to the seventh chapter of Revelation). This is outright blasphemy, because they made God, the very highest and holiest authority there is, be the originator and confirmer of false doctrine. Satan, a created being, and who is called the god of this world, is the one who originates and seeks to confirm false doctrine by twisting God's Word, *not* the Most High.

"A Mark" Turns into "The Mark"

Finally the authors got to the point where they chose a specific name for the cross-shaped smudge. They already warmed up the reader to the idea by having the doctor say he saw "a mark" on Buck's forehead. Next, they wrote into the story a time where the characters called the seal "the mark:"

> "That's the sign of the sealed servants of God! You have one too, so I know you're a believer. Right?"
> "Praise God!" the doctor said. "I am, but I don't think I have the mark."
> We can't see our own! Only others'." (*Soul Harvest*, p. 195)
>
> Buck saw the mark on her forehead and smiled, wondering if she was aware of it yet. (*Soul Harvest*, p. 200)

Visible "Mark of the Believer" is Not in the Bible

The authors slowly developed the story to the point where God gave all the Christian characters visible marks on their foreheads. They chose the phrase "the mark" to name this allegedly visible sealing. This phrase, with the meaning "a mark in one's body," does not exist in the New Testament except to denote the mark of the beast. The Bible also uses "a mark" or "his mark" to refer to the mark of the beast as well (see Rev. 13:17, Rev. 14:11, Rev. 16:2, Rev. 19:20).

In the New Testament, the phrase, "the mark," refers to holiness only one time:

> I press toward the mark for the prize of the high calling of God in Christ Jesus. (Phil. 3:14)

"The mark" means "goal" in this scripture. Pressing toward the mark is biblical; knowing our brother by his "mark" is not.

Uniting the Holy and the Profane

Calling this fictional visible seal "the mark" links together by word association the holy (the Christian) and the profane (the follower of Antichrist). God's people are called to be holy and *must* know the difference between the holy and the profane, and be able to discern between the clean and the unclean (see Ezek. 44:23). The authors have used the name for the profane ("the mark") and united this unholy phrase with God's holy people. With God there is no mixture of light and darkness:

> ... God is light, and in Him is no darkness at all. (1 John 1:5)

The same God who has no darkness in Him at all will not use the name of Satan's seal of ownership and use it to describe something He put on His own beloved children.

Tsion Ben-Judah Preached There is No Question Who the True Believers Are

The authors want the readers of their book series to think that the Bible teaches there will be a visible seal on Christians' foreheads that will enable them to have a reliable way of knowing who is one of them and who is not. They again used the spiritual authority figure – Tsion Ben-Judah – to write an internet sermon about this subject:

> Is that not a wonderful and most blessed promise? Revelation 7 indicates that the trumpet judgments I just mentioned will not come until the servants of God have been sealed on their foreheads. There will no longer be any question who the true believers are. (*Soul Harvest*, p. 248)
>
> Just within the last several hours, it has become clear to me and to other brothers and sisters in Christ that the seal on the forehead of the true believer is already visible, but apparently only to other believers. This was a thrilling discovery, and I look forward to hearing from many of you who detect it on each other. (*Soul Harvest*, pp. 248-49)

Have Mark, Have Salvation?

This is the main point of the whole "mark of the believer" false doctrine that started in *Soul Harvest* and was repeated several times in each subsequent book. The Christian reader, and also the reader that has not yet surrendered his life in faith to the Lord Jesus Christ for salvation, is literally being programmed to think that during the tribulation, real Christians will have cross-shaped smudge marks on their foreheads. The false doctrine of the cross-shaped mark is being presented to the reader as the litmus test to determine the authenticity of a person's salvation.

Here is an example in *Soul Harvest* where "the mark" means Christian, even without a confession of the Lord Jesus Christ:

> "So that's what's different?" Buck said.
> "That, and this." Ken ran his hand through his hair again, and this time left it atop his head with his hair pulled out of the way. "Maybe it shows on my forehead. I can see yours. Can you see mine?" (*Soul Harvest*, p. 314)

According to the *Left Behind* series, Christians will definitely be able to safely entrust themselves to any person having a visible cross on his forehead. They need never be concerned about falling into the hands of pseudo-Christians who are really Antichrist's people in disguise. They will know the genuine article simply by seeing "the mark of the believer." But wait... what about those who might try to *fake* "the mark of the believer"?

Testing the Mark of the Believer For Authenticity

As with all propagandist literature, the questions and objections of the reader are always addressed in the storyline. The reader is probably wondering whether someone could perhaps simply paint a mark on his forehead to look just like the "mark of the believer" described in the *Left Behind* series. If this question is not addressed in the story, the reader will not be completely convinced that seeing "the mark of the believer" on a person's forehead is a guarantee they are really a Christian. Perhaps true believers will not be able to know each other on sight after all.

Rayford Steele was having a very difficult time trusting Albie because he was so convincing in his pose as a GC commander. Albie was terribly insulted that he was being judged by his fruits and kept insisting that Rayford check his "mark:"

> "Take it as a compliment, Albie. If you're for real, you were so convincing as a GC commander that you made me wonder." (*The Indwelling*, p. 376)

This is exactly the same thing as saying that a Christian was convincing as a high-level satanist, but the authors never made it plain to the reader that that the GC are actually satanists.

Albie grew weary of not being taken for a true Christian even while acting like a GC commander:

> "Hadn't you better check me to see if you signed the death warrants of all your friends? Or will you risk their lives to keep from insulting me further?" (*The Indwelling*, p. 378)

> Albie took a step closer, making Rayford flinch, but Albie merely stuck his forehead in Rayford's face.
> "Touch it, rub it, wash it, put petrol on it. Do whatever you have to do to convince yourself. I already know who I am. If I'm phony, shoot me." (*The Indwelling*, p. 378)

Through this dialogue, the reader is led to believe there is a way a Christian can test whether a person's "mark of the believer" is real or phony. If it does not wash off, it is a real "mark." This is not harmless entertainment; it is propaganda that is designed to shape the minds and attitudes of the masses, and it is extremely dangerous.

The "mark of the believer" teaching is repeated in all the books in the *Left Behind* series subsequent to *Soul Harvest*. The propaganda technique of repetition was heavily utilized to saturate the reader with this false doctrine.

"The Mark of the Believer" Doctrine Is Deadly to the Christian

This doctrine is not in the Bible, but was presented as a Bible doctrine in the *Left Behind* series. The reader has the example of relativism presented to him as being the way to understand the Bible. If certain events occur (people disappear, or a Christian receives the mark of the beast unwillingly, or people are seen with crosses on their foreheads that will not wash off) the reader is directed to Bible verses that he has been led to believe back up these occurrences even though they do not teach them. This is New Age relativism.

Any Christian or Christian-to-be who takes "the mark of the believer" doctrine seriously is being set up to disbelieve his own standing in the Lord and also the standing of those he has trusted for years as brothers or sisters in the Lord. At a time when Christians will need to trust and help each other *more than at any other time in history*, the false doctrine of the "mark of the believer" will cause them to not be able to trust even their own fellow brothers and sisters in Christ, because no true Christian will have a cross-shaped mark on his forehead.

The Lord Jesus Christ told us we will know true Christians by their fruit, and that no good tree brings forth corrupt fruit. "Ye shall know them by their fruits" (see Matt. 7:15-17). The Bible also says that those whose true foundation is in the Lord have this seal in their *behavior*:

> Nevertheless the foundation of God standeth sure, having this seal, The Lord knoweth them that are his. And let every-one that nameth the name of Christ depart from iniquity. (2 Tim. 2:19)

The *Left Behind* series contradicted the Lord Jesus Christ's command to "know them by their fruits." They also provided an example in *Apollyon* where a person with a profession of faith in Jesus Christ was lying and therefore not Christ-like. Rayford knew he was lying, but still believed he was a Christian because he could see "the mark" on his forehead. It was not until Rayford realized that an unbeliever named Bo could actually see the

"Christian liar's" mark that he knew Ernie was not a real Christian. This is blatantly teaching the reader to *not* know them by their fruits, but only by their marks:

> Rayford was disgusted with Ernie's obvious lies but even more so that he was ashamed of the mark of God. And then it hit him. Only other believers could see the mark. Was Rayford arguing with a fellow tribulation saint? He looked quickly at Bo's forehead, which, because of his complexion and the breadth of his face, had been right in front of Rayford's eyes the whole time.
> Even in the dense fog, Bo's face was as clear as a baby's. (*Apollyon*, p. 302)
>
> Rayford grabbed Ernie by the collar and pulled him close, feeling the rage of a parent against a threat to his family.
> "So you're an imposter, hey, Ernie?" (*Apollyon*, p. 311)

Another reason the "mark of the believer" teaching is a deadly doctrine is this: because true Christians will not have any visible mark; the only ones who will have it will be people *posing* as Christians. In the following example, Ernie was shown to fake the "mark of the believer," and the authors had Rayford say something very interesting to him:

> "You'd fake the mark, Ernie? The mark of the sealed of the Lord? That takes guts.
> Ernie paled and tried to pull away, but Rayford grabbed the back of his neck and with his free hand pressed his thumb against Ernie's bogus mark. The smudge rubbed off. "You must have studied Tsion's teaching really well to replicate a mark you've never seen."
> (*Apollyon*, pp. 311-12)

The authors had Rayford say it took guts to fake the mark of the sealed of the Lord. It will *not* take guts for satanists to pose as Christians during the tribulation and to tattoo on their foreheads crosses that will not wash off. It will *not* take guts for these agents of Satan to make money and gain rank in Satan's kingdom by luring Christians (as well as Jews and others) to their death through this guise. Besides destroying the faith of Christians, the "mark of the believer" doctrine will enable satanists to pose as Christians and be assured of instant acceptance by anyone deceived by this false doctrine taught in the *Left Behind* series. If the "mark of the believer" ruse is not exposed far and wide, it will be easy for "marked" fake Christians to lead New World Order resistors to their death.

This is because a true Christian will help a non-Christian if he is hungry and thirsty and needs shelter. This occurred during the Holocaust when Christian families risked their lives to help the oppressed Jewish people. Any Jew (or any other person determined not to accept the occult religion of the New Age) who reads this series and believes that real Christians will have cross marks on their foreheads during the coming time of intense persecution is being set up to trust satanist imposters who will exterminate them as dissidents.

Satanists posing as Christians are heavily integrated into the churches *right now* and get away with it for the precise reason advocated in the *Left Behind* series. Christians are not presently obeying the Lord Jesus and "knowing" their brothers and sisters by their fruits, but accept them as brethren by their profession, their scripture knowledge, their appearance, and their money.

Test of an Antichrist Person

Satanists in leadership positions in the church know the Bible very well and have learned how to use it to their master's advantage to pervert the Christian from the right way of the Lord. Bible knowledge is *not* the test of a true Christian. Wolves in sheep's clothing will even say "Jesus Christ is Lord." That is also not the test of an antichrist person. Even the devils believe that Jesus Christ is the Lord. What an antichrist Christian pretender will *not* do is confess with their mouth and *with their life* that "Jesus Christ is *their own* Lord."

Remember, anyone can "talk the talk." Satan knows the Bible and instructs his followers in how to use it for *his* purposes in the church. His false teachers work to subvert God's people and speed up the falling away. These pretenders will not walk with Jesus Christ but will only confess Him with their mouth as the Lord. Their lives reveal their *real* lord.

Satan's followers *always* give themselves away by their fruits even if only in subtle ways, so "the mark of the believer" doctrine is a gift to them straight from hell. It will help them greatly in furthering their agenda of rounding up and disposing of multitudes of Christian hold-outs who will have the presence of mind to hide as soon as they hear the first word about any disappearances.

The "mark of the believer" doctrine is antichrist. It *replaces* the test Jesus gave to His disciples (knowing them by their fruits) with a doctrine of devils. Renounce this devilish doctrine in the name of Jesus Christ

9

SATAN ON THE MARK OF THE BEAST

Right from the first book in the series the writers promoted new, unbiblical teachings about the mark of the beast. Of course they used an authority figure, Bruce Barnes, to do this. First, Bruce explained to newly converted Chloe the vulnerabilities of Christians during the Tribulation, the time of Antichrist's reign.

> "There will come a time, Chloe, that followers of Antichrist will be required to bear the sign of the beast." (*Left Behind*, pp. 420-21)

He then went on to explain that there were many theories about what form it might take.

> "But obviously we would refuse to bear that mark. That very act of defiance will be a mark in itself. We will be the naked ones, the ones devoid of the protection of belonging to the majority." (*Left Behind*, p. 421)

Bruce told Chloe that the act of defiance toward taking the mark of the beast would be a mark (of God) in itself. He failed to say that confessing Jesus Christ before men – and therefore getting victory over the mark – is the mark of being a real Christian.

No Mark: Nakedness and No Protection

Next, let us look at a message in the following passage:

> "But obviously we would refuse to bear that mark. That very act of defiance will be a mark in itself. We will be the naked ones, the ones devoid of the protection of belonging to the majority." (*Left Behind*, p. 421)

Bruce equated not having the mark of the beast as being in the state of being *naked,* and *"devoid of the protection* of the majority." The authors had this authority figure make two negative remarks about not having the mark of the beast. They had Bruce Barnes say that as Christians, we would be the "naked ones" and "devoid of the protection of the majority."

He did not say that God would *protect* faithful Christians and that no overcoming Christian will ever desire Antichrist's soul-damning "protection" no matter how much of a price they have to pay to be true to Jesus Christ. The message being sent here is that conforming to the beast's demands equals protection, and conforming to the image of Christ equals no protection.

In the next section, you will see the authors put positive connotations upon having the mark of the beast. This is not accidental. They *chose* to use these print subliminals to connect *not* having the mark of the beast with *negative* words, and having the mark of the beast with positive words.

Yes, in much of the "right out in front of you" kind of writing they depicted the mark of the beast as something that is dangerous and to be avoided by the Christian. However, it is necessary to bring to your attention the places where the authors sent pro-mark-of-the-beast messages to you by the use of manipulative writing so that you may pass judgment upon them according to the Word of God. Remember the Bible warning:

> A little leaven leaveneth the whole lump. (Gal. 5:9)

The authors used more than a little leaven to leaven the *Left Behind* series and their non-fiction books with false, relativistic mark-of-the-beast teachings.

Take the Mark and Live as a Free Man

> "I pledge this to you as I did once before to Tsion," Chaim said. "I will not take the mark of Nicolae Carpathia. If I should starve to death for taking that stand, I shall not be forced to bear a mark in order to live as a free man in this society." (*Assassins,* p. 271)

The writers had Chaim say what Lucifer (Satan) wants everyone to think. He wants everyone to think that appeasing him by taking his mark is freedom.

> Lucifer comes to give us the final gift of wholeness. If we accept it, then he is free and we are free. That is the Luciferic initiation. It is one that many people now, and in the days ahead, will be facing, for it is an initiation into the New Age.[1]

Conforming to an established pattern, the authors chose to use a positive word in connection to something connected with Satan. The word "free," used in association with the mark of the beast, was also used in Chang's remarks about the benefits of having the mark after it was forced upon him:

> "Therefore, I am free to live among them – buy and sell, come and go, even work here – without suspicion and – if I'm careful – without risk." (*The Mark*, p. 356)

Defiance is a Mark of God?

Chang was a seventeen year-old teenager who was a secret follower of Jesus. He was brought to Antichrist's palace for Carpathia's funeral and to be interviewed for a job position. When his father made it clear to him that he was to take the mark of the beast in order to work for Antichrist, Chang adamantly refused to take the mark. His father came up to him at one point and gave him a tranquilizing shot, which drugged him into submission. His father and Mr. Moon then dragged Chang away to be forcibly marked. While Chang was losing consciousness he continued to insist he would not take the mark, and finally crossed himself. This was a demonstration of the doctrine of "defiance is a mark in itself" taught in the first book of the *Left Behind* series. Chang was defiant but he did not follow the Lord Jesus Christ merely by being defiant about taking the mark:

> And he said to them all, If any man will come after me, let him deny himself, and take up his cross daily, and follow me. For whosoever will save his life shall lose it: but whosoever will lose his life for my sake, the same shall save it. (Luke 9:23-24)

He denied the Lord Jesus by putting his own physical safety and that of his sister Ming before his loyalty to the Lord Jesus Christ. Chang did not come after Jesus on Jesus' own terms and therefore was not a true Christian.

Chang Had a Choice to Confess Jesus

Yes, Chang had a choice to actually *follow* Jesus once he had believed upon His name. Instead of following Jesus and enduring to the end, as must all overcomers, he compromised from the very beginning by refusing to confess to his father that he had decided to follow Jesus. He had ample time to confess the Lord Jesus Christ before his father, thinking him merely contrary, drugged him and carried him away to receive the mark which is for non-confessors of the Lord Jesus Christ.

The storyline had Chang *not confessing Jesus Christ* and thereby saving his own physical life in this world, as well as that of his sister, Ming. The justification made in the storyline for Chang being unwilling to admit to being a Christian was that he wanted to keep his Christian sister "safe" to continue serving in Antichrist's regime undetected. If he was found out to be a "Judahite," both he and Ming would be martyred for their faith.

Even when his father insisted that he take the mark of the beast, Chang remained silent about his supposed devotion to Jesus Christ. His father actually told Chang,

> "And now we know the potentate is the son of god!" Chang replied, "He is not! I know no such thing! He could be the son of Satan for all I know!" (*Desecration,* p. 63)

Chang had the opportunity and the *obligation* to counter this blasphemy by confessing Jesus Christ as the Son of God, but instead, he denied Christ by his silence about being His follower. He did not even forthrightly renounce Antichrist for what he really was, but merely said "He could be he son of Satan for all I know!" He would not accept the consequences that come to Christians who are patient during times of tribulation. Make no mistake: Chang *chose* to deny the Lord Jesus Christ by his silence, and those who deny Jesus Christ will be denied by Him before His Father in heaven.

David Commended Chang For Losing the Testimony of Jesus

Back in the book, *The Mark,* the authors had the character named David *commend* Chang for not making it known that he belonged to Christ:

> "I'm glad you didn't just scream out that you're a believer."
> (*The Mark,* p. 353)

Losing the testimony of Jesus *is* submission to Satan. David, a Christian, commended Chang for losing the testimony of Jesus. This is one of the many reasons Satan is the "God" of the *Left Behind* series.

A Christian Will Be *Unable* to Take the Mark?

The false doctrine the authors had Tsion Ben-Judah teach the reader through his internet sermon is one of the most dangerous false teachings in the *Left Behind* series. They actually had this Bible teacher character address a major concern of the reader and give a bogus answer that sets the reader up to be cast into the lake of fire.

First, the authors had Tsion's internet sermon address to the website reader the same concerns of the reader of *The Mark*:

> Many have written in fear, confessing that they do not believe they have the courage to choose death over life when threatened with the guillotine. As a fellow pilgrim in this journey of faith, let me admit that I do not understand this either. In my flesh I am weak. I want to live. I am afraid of death but even more of dying. (*The Mark,* p. 338)

Tsion began by identifying with the reader's problem. He admitted that he was afraid of death and dying:

> I envision myself breaking God's heart by denying my Lord. Oh, what an awful picture! (*The Mark,* p. 338

Tsion equated denying his Lord with breaking God's heart. Indeed it would be so, but the writers did *not* have this character explain the consequences if a Christian denies Christ before men.

"For there is one God, and one mediator between God and men, the man Christ Jesus" (1 Tim. 2:5)

Jesus is our mediator, but if we lose the testimony of Jesus by denying Him before men in order to save our own lives in this world, He will not longer mediate, but instead, He will deny us:

But whosoever shall deny me before men, him will I also deny before my Father which is in heaven. (Matt. 10:33)

In my most hated imagination I fail at the hour of testing and accept the mark of loyalty that we all know is the cursed mark of the beast, all because I so cherish my own life. (*The Mark,* pp. 338-39)

Here is another false teaching slipped into Tsion's internet sermon. Tsion wrote that he cherished his own life. This is the opposite of what true Christianity is all about, and it also contradicts what a Christian needs to do to be able to overcome the beast. Tsion's sermon had an antichrist agenda sent directly to the reader.

He that loveth his life shall lose it; and he that hateth his life in this world shall keep it unto life. (John 12:25)

And they overcame him by the blood of the Lamb, and by the word of their testimony; and they loved not their lives unto the death. (Rev. 12:11)

Christians are commanded by the Lord Jesus to hate their own lives in this world. To cherish our lives is to go directly against the words of Jesus Christ, and is antichrist. Not loving your own life is one of the three main ways a Christian overcomes Antichrist. The authors took away all three of these ways to defeat Antichrist in the storyline.

Tsion repeated the reader's fear about denying Christ:

But have you a foreboding about that day when you will be forced to publicly declare your faith or deny your Savior? (*The Mark,* p. 339)

This is the second time the authors brought up the "denying Christ"' theme without mentioning the consequences. Tsion continues with a soul-damning partial truth for the reader:

> The Bible tells us that once one is either sealed by God as a believer or accept the mark of loyalty to Antichrist, this is a once-and-for-all choice. In other words, if you have decided for Christ and the seal of God is evident on your forehead, you cannot change your mind! (*The Mark*, p. 339)

The *true* part of Tsion's statement is that once you have taken the mark of the beast, it is a no-turning-back situation. Whoever takes the mark of the beast seals his own fate for an eternity and will be forever tormented in the lake of fire.

The *false* part of Tsion's statement is that once you have decided for Christ you cannot change your mind. This is dangerous and antibiblical, and it sets the reader up to lose his own soul if he believes it.

The authors had Tsion repeat this lie, while italicizing the word "unable" twice to make sure the reader believes the diabolical point:

> That tells me somehow, when we face the ultimate test, God miraculously overcomes our evil, selfish flesh and gives us the grace and courage to make the right decision in spite of our-selves. My interpretation of this is that we will be *unable* to deny Jesus, *unable* to even choose the mark that would temporarily save our lives. (*The Mark*, p. 339)

The "authority character" Tsion Ben-Judah was used to perpetrate the lie that if a Christian finds himself in the position of being required to take the take the mark of the beast, he would be *unable* to deny Jesus and *unable* to even choose to take the mark.

This is a strange statement in view of the number of times the members of the Tribulation Force denied Christ, even though the narration never indicated this is what they were actually doing. The statement, "We will be unable to deny Jesus" is *antichrist,* because it is against the words of the Lord Jesus Christ:

> But whosoever shall deny me before men, him will I also deny before my Father which is in heaven. (Matt. 10:33)

Jesus spoke these words to His twelve disciples. Christians, disciples of Jesus Christ, have the ability to deny Jesus Christ before men. The reason they are tempted to do this is to save their own lives in this world. Jesus also told them that if they love their own life in this world they will lose their eternal life:

> He that loveth his life shall lose it; and he that hateth his life in this world shall keep it unto life eternal. (John 12:25)

Jesus Christ said denying Him before men *is* possible, and He said that if we love our own life in this world we will lose it. Denying Christ is not for the lost. They cannot deny him because they have never owned him. Christians must beware of denying the Lord Jesus Christ and most importantly, beware of false teachers who tell you that God will make you unable to deny Christ, and unable to take the mark of the beast.

Just as God did not render Adam and Eve unable to choose to eat the fruit of the tree of knowledge of good and evil, God will not overcome us and make us unable to take the mark of the beast. The grace to get victory over the mark is covered in the chapter entitled "The Bible on the Mark of the Beast."

Mark of the Beast On Forehead or Hand?

> Someday, according to Bruce's teaching, to merely have the right to buy and sell, citizens of the Global Community would have to take "the mark of the beast." No one knew yet exactly what form this would take, but the Bible indicated it would be a mark on the forehead or on the hand. There would be no faking. The mark would be specifically detectable. (*Nicolae*, pp. 285-86)

The Holy Bible indicates the mark of the beast will be *in,* not *on,* the forehead or hand:

> And the third angel followed them, saying with a loud voice, If any man worship the beast and his image, and receive his mark in his forehead, or in his hand,
> The same shall drink of the wine of the wrath of God, which is poured out without mixture into the cup of his indignation; and he shall be tormented with fire and brimstone in the presence of the holy angels, and in the presence of the Lamb. (Rev.14:9,10)

Two Books of Life: Doctrine of Apostasy

Before the authors wrote Chang's forced marking into the storyline, they prepared the reader to accept this lie with the false two books of life teaching. This false doctrine is also in Tim LaHaye's nonfiction books.[2,3]

The authors used the propaganda technique of "appeal to authority" to help ensure the reader would believe this false doctrine.

> Appeal to Authority. Appeals to authority cite prominent figures to support a position idea, argument, or course of action.[4]

This "appeal to authority" technique was used many times in the series: Tsion did not tell Chloe she would lose her soul if she killed her son and herself; Tsion reassured Chang he was still saved after being marked with the beast; Tsion is the person who had two out-of-body experiences and spoke to spirit guides ("angels"), etc.

This was a widely-used propaganda technique to lend credence to doctrines and experiences they especially wanted the reader to believe. Tsion closed an internet sermon with these words:

> My next message will concern the difference between the Book of Life and the Lamb's Book of Life, and what those mean to you and me. Until then, you may rest assured that if you are a believer and have placed your hope and trust in the work of Jesus Christ alone for the forgiveness of sins and for life everlasting, your name is in the Lamb's Book of Life.
> And it can never be erased. (*The Mark*, p. 149)

Immediately the reader wonders what could Tsion possibly mean? There are *two* books of life? The authors had Buck, with whom the reader vicariously identifies with, wonder the same thing:

> And a difference between the Book of Life and the Lamb's Book of Life? He had never heard of such a thing and couldn't wait to learn more. (*The Mark*, p. 150)

If the reader is a Christian, he wonders one more thing: It can never be erased? Jesus said *overcomers* were not blotted out of the book of life:

> He that overcometh, the same shall be clothed in white raiment; and I will not blot out his name out of the book of life, but I will confess his name before my Father, and before his angels. (Rev. 3:5)

Jesus said these words to the church at Sardis, not to the world. He will not blot out the name of the Christian that overcomes, but Tsion, the Bible scholar said that a believer can never be erased from the Lamb's book of life.

Jesus not only said that he who overcomes will not be blotted out of the book of life, he even defined overcomer so that there is no misunderstanding:

> And he that overcometh, and keepeth my works unto the end, to him will I give power over the nations. (Rev. 2:26)

An overcomer, according to the Lord Jesus Christ, is the Christian who keeps His works unto the end. The overcomer will not be blotted out of the book of life. The Tribulation Force did not keep Jesus works unto the end. The fact that they were near the end (in the tribulation) was the very excuse the authors gave in the storyline for these characters to not overcome. Let us examine what Tsion did to try to twist the scriptures to fit the heresy that "a believer cannot be erased from the book of life."

Tsion first cited the scripture verses he was going to say did not mean what they said:

> Exodus 32:33 says, "And the Lord said to Moses, 'Whosoever has sinned against Me, I will blot him out of My book.'"
> These references naturally have caused some to fear that they can lose their salvation. But my contention is that the book referred to in those is the book of God the Father, into which are written the names of every person he created. (*The Mark,* p. 342)

Tsion said it is his contention and that part is right. It is Tsion's argument, not the teaching of scripture, that the book referred to in Exodus 32:33 is a book in which the lost and saved are written.

This is a new and untrue doctrine that is antichrist because it directly opposes the doctrine of Jesus Christ.

Tsion went on to say there is another book of life, but this one is called the Book of Life of the Lamb. I will cite the verse here:

> And all that dwell upon the earth shall worship him, whose names are not written in the book of life of the Lamb slain from the foundation of the world. (Rev. 13:8)

The Bible does not teach there are two books of life, but that did not deter Tsion from his antichrist teaching.

> The most important difference between these two books is that it is clear a person can have his name blotted out of the Book of the Living. But in Revelation 3:5, Jesus himself promises, "He who overcomes shall be clothed in white garments, and I will not blot out his name from the Book of Life; but I will confess his name before My Father and before His angels." (*The Mark*, p. 343)

This is the verse that has to be made to mean something different than it says for Tsion to promote his unconditional security teaching. Tsion skirted the condition of being an overcomer:

> The overcomers he is referring to are those clothed in the white garments of Christ himself, guaranteeing that their names cannot be blotted out of the Book of Life of the Lamb. (*The Mark*, p. 343)

Tsion rearranged the verse to make it say what he wanted it to say. The verse really says "he who overcomes shall be clothed in white garments" but Tsion made it say "the overcomers are clothed in the white garments thus guaranteeing they cannot be blotted out of the Book of Life of the Lamb." Tsion took Jesus' conditional promise and made it unconditional.

This is so satanic and reminds me of what Satan communicated through the serpent to Eve. His message to her was that God's promises are unconditional even though He clearly put a condition on them ("Ye shall not surely die"). Eve was deceived into thinking God did not mean what he said, and the readers of the *Left Behind* series must not follow suit. God *does* mean what He says, and an overcomer is a certain kind of Christian. He is one who keeps Jesus' works until the end.

Tsion's ruse has been exposed, but I will simply complete this by mentioning that he told the reader that God only blots people out of a certain book called the Book of the Living. He said the people who get blotted out are people who die without becoming Christians.

> But those who have trusted Christ have been written in the Lamb's Book of Life, so that when they die physically, they remain alive spiritually and are never blotted out. (*The Mark*, p. 343)

This is diametrically opposed to the teaching of the Lord Jesus Christ. This is antichrist teaching and will send many to hell if they think only the lost can be blotted out of the book of life. This is such a perversion, which is why it is so satanic. Satan perverts and turns inside out as many things of God as he can. Bible fact: only Christians can be blotted out of the book of life. Satanic perversion: Only unbelievers can be blotted out of the book of life.

Sin *Can* Separate Us From the Love of Christ

The authors had Chang say,

> "The Bible says nothing can separate us from the love of Christ, and that has to include our own selves." (*The Mark*, p. 354)

That sounds like a nice thought but it directly contradicts the Holy Bible. Christians are commanded to

> Keep yourselves in the love of God, looking for the mercy of our Lord Jesus Christ unto eternal life. (Jude 1:21)

The love of God is keeping his word:

> But whoso keepeth his word, in him verily is the love of God perfected: hereby know we that we are in him. (1 John 2:5)

Christians keep themselves in the love of God and know they are in Him as they keep His word. The authors are trying to get the reader to think that even having the mark of the beast will not separate a Christian from the love of God! Let us look at the verses Chang referred to when he said, "Nothing can separate us from the love of Christ; and that has to include our own selves."

> Who shall separate us from the love of Christ? Shall tribulation, or distress, or persecution, or famine, or nakedness, or peril or sword?
> As it is written, For thy sake we are killed all the day long; we are accounted as sheep for the slaughter.
> Nay, in all these things we are more than conquerors through him that loved us.
> For I am persuaded, that neither death, nor life, nor angels, nor principalities, nor powers, nor things present, nor things to come,
> Nor height, nor depth, nor any other creature, shall be able to separate us from the love of God, which is in Christ Jesus our Lord. (Rom. 8:35-39)

Paul wrote that *in all* these things we are more than conquerors through Him that loved us. Chang was not a conqueror in these things. He was conquered, or overcome. The true Christian faith is the victory that overcomes the world. The "not being separated from the love of God" promise is for the Christian: the one who counts himself as a sheep for the slaughter (rather than deny Christ) and is a conqueror over sin and the world through Him that loved us. Every promise in the Bible comes with a condition, and the "nothing shall separate us from the love of God" promise is no exception.

Christians With Both Marks Are In a Special Category?

In response to Chang's query about his present spiritual status now that he has both marks, David replied,

> "As for what you are, with both marks you surely have to be in a special category." (*The Mark*, p. 353)

Of course this does not sit well with the Christian reader who knows that he cannot serve two masters, nor be marked by two masters either. The authors anticipated this resistance to their new "mark of the beast paradigm shift" and used Chang to voice the objections the reader has with this answer:

> "But all that stuff Dr. Ben-Judah writes about, choosing between the seal of God and the mark of the beast. I chose, and I got both. Now what?" (*The Mark*, p. 353)

The authors attempted to have the reader buy the idea that Chang chose God but ended up with Satan's mark anyway. There is supposedly a special category of Christian who loves the Lord Jesus Christ, but has the mark forced upon him. This category does not exist in the Bible – or really even in the book, because Chang did *not* choose the Lord Jesus Christ. He *denied* Him by keeping completely silent about his Christian beliefs because he was not willing to face the persecutions that those who live godly in Christ Jesus face.

Even while his powers of speech were rapidly slipping away under the effects of the tranquilizing drug, Chang did not say the words, Jesus Christ. He only crossed himself, which is *not* a non-verbal confession of Bible Christianity, but only of Catholicism.

Advantages to Having the Mark of the Beast Forced Upon a Christian?

The fact that the authors chose to insert the blasphemous "plot twist" of a Christian being marked with the beast into what is supposed to be Christian fiction is bad enough, but what is even worse is that they had Chang, who refused to confess the Lord Jesus Christ and ended up forcibly marked as a result, speak of advantages to having Satan's mark of allegiance:

> "I didn't choose the mark. It was forced on me. I see nothing but benefits." (*The Mark*, p. 354)

> "I don't have to like it, but what's done is done, and a smart guy like you ought to be able to see the upside of this." (*The Mark*, p. 354)

> "What are you going to do with the 'advantage,' as you call it, being bi-loyal for lack of a better term?" (*The Mark*, p. 355)

"First, I like the term. Bi-loyal. That's the way it appears." (*The Mark*, p. 355)

The reader gets the impression that Chang's dilemma is not a dilemma at all, and that since "what's done is done," Chang might as well make the best of it. Also, notice the authors' continued use of the word association technique of connecting positive words with the mark of the beast: "benefits," "upside," and "advantage."

Tsion Had No Idea Why Chang Was Suicidal

Dr. Tsion Ben Judah received an email from Chang with the message, "I am despairing for my life." This is quite normal considering that Chang had the mark of the beast, and he knew what the Bible teaches is the fate of *any* who have it.

Tsion responded,

> "I am here, young brother. I know you must feel very much alone, but do not despair. The Lord is with you. He will give his angels charge over you. You have much to do as the point man for all the various activities of the Tribulation Force around the world. Yes, it is probably too much to ask of one so young, in years and in the faith, but we all must do what we have to. Tell me how I can encourage and help you so you can return to the task." (*Desecration*, p. 9)

Now Tsion knew full well that Chang had the mark of the beast (and had written about the consequences of being marked with the beast's mark on his internet website) but the authors had this character misunderstand the intent of Chang's desperate note. Tsion was made out to be thinking that Chang's worry was that he could not handle his assignment in the Tribulation Force.

Chang responded,

> "I want to kill myself." (*Desecration*, p. 9)

Again, Tsion is shown to misunderstand Chang's desperate statement, thus lessening the importance of Chang's very real peril in the minds of the readers.

> "Chang! Unless you have purposely jeopardized our mission, you need feel no such remorse. If you have made a mistake, reveal it so we can all adapt." (*Desecration*, p. 9)

Even after Chang made the statement, "I want to kill myself" Tsion, the spiritual mentor of the Tribulation Force, still had no idea this had anything to do with the mark of the beast in Chang's body. This is absurd, but the authors used Tsion's clueless state about the reason for Chang's distress to lessen the importance, in the reader's mind, of Chang having Satan's mark.

Tsion continued to emphasize Chang's *physical* task:

> "But you have satellites to manipulate and monitor. You have records to keep in order, in case the enemy checks the various aliases and operations. We are nearly at zero hour, so do not lose heart. You can do this." (*Desecration*, p. 9)

Chang responded about his assignment and as a closing statement said,

> "I could end my life right now and not affect the Tribulation Force." (*Desecration*, p. 9)

Tsion, *again,* was oblivious as to the reason for the anguish in the heart of his "marked with the beast" Christian brother:

> "Stop this talk, Chang! We need you. You must stay in position and adjust the databases depending upon what we encounter. Now, quickly, please, what is the problem?" (*Desecration*, p. 9)

The authors manipulated to the maximum to de-emphasize the seriousness and gravity of a Christian having the mark of the beast. The authors then used David and other characters to send the message to the reader that a Christian bearing the mark of the beast is not that important:

> David set his machine on the seat and stood outside, leaning in. The others stretched, then gathered to hear him read Tsion's copy of

his back-and-forth with Chang. "That does not sound so good," Abdullah said. "What to do?"
I'd take a tone with that boy," Mac said.
"Just what I was thinking," David said. (*Desecration*, pp. 19-20)

Three more Christian characters minimized Chang's biblically correct fears about being marked with Satan's own identifying mark. The reader is seeing the characters agreeing that Chang needs to be rebuked because he is not sticking to temporal things and is instead focusing upon the evil mark of Satan in his body.

David emailed a letter of rebuke to Chang:

"You've got time to interrupt Dr. Ben Judah but not to check in with your immediate superior?" (*Desecration*, p. 20)

This is yet another opportunity for the authors' to attach little importance to Chang's situation of being yoked to Satan eternally through the mark of the beast. It was right for Chang to contact Dr. Ben-Judah first because he is considered to be the most godly and spiritual man in the Tribulation Force. The authors' portrayal of David being angry and considering Chang's desperate email to Tsion an "interruption, is one more way the writers manipulated the story to get the reader to dismiss the seriousness of Chang's predicament in the readers' minds.

David said:

"You think this is a game, Chang?" (*Desecration*, p. 20)

The authors again endeavored to persuade the reader that Chang's spiritual dilemma is really no dilemma at all, and that Chang's grief and suicidal feelings about having the mark that will put him in smoke and torment forever are merely childish games:

"What happened to the smart-aleck know-it-all who was going to handle all this in his sleep? Nobody begrudges you your second thoughts and spiritual angst, but you had better come to grips that you accepted this assignment." (*Desecration*, p. 20)

Now we have David conceding that perhaps Chang *does* have the right to some second thoughts about whether having the mark would be advantageous. But David also told Chang that since he accepted the assignment of working for the Tribulation Force, he had better stay focused on it, as it pertained to the *physical* survival of the group, and stop this foolish preoccupation with the state of his soul.

David continued to reprove Chang:

> "Bottom line, Chang, is that you don't have time for this right now." (*Desecration*, p. 20)

Here is *another* time the authors worked through David's character to urge the reader to believe a Christian's distress about being yoked with Satan through the mark is insignificant compared to the temporal matters at hand:

> "Doing harm to yourself because you can't figure out why God might have let something happen would be the most royally selfish act you could conjure up." (*Desecration*, p. 20)

The reader is now led to believe that God let "something happen." God is the one who let Chang be marked with the beast – and remain saved? God is being made the one who is responsible for the circumstances that led to Chang's forced marking. The only "God" who would do that is Satan! We see another example of why Satan is the "God" of the *Left Behind* series. If Chang did not keep silent about his faith in Jesus Christ, then the whole incident, including all the manipulation of the reader's mind, could have never been written into the story.

Next, the reader is led to believe that if Chang commits suicide over this spiritual tragedy, it would be the most royally selfish act he could conjure up. Yes, suicide is selfish, and is a sin for which there is no repentance, and therefore must never be committed. However, the authors used the propaganda device of repetition to get across the notion that Chang should dismiss the fact that he has the mark of the beast and just get on with the task of serving in Antichrist's employ.

The story then continues with David reminding Chang of his responsibilities on the job. Now that the authors have worked hard through the character of David to convince the reader that a

Christian having the mark of the beat is no big deal, they used this same character to address Chang's "dual mark" problem.

I will pick up with the contents of the email where David is again referring to Chang's mark of the beast problem:

> "Hear me, Chang. Something you wrote to Dr. Ben-Judah reminded me of something you said to me about this whole dual mark thing. I know you didn't take it on purpose, though you wanted me to think you got used to it right away and see, as you called it, the 'upside.' " (*Desecration*, p. 21)

The "dual mark thing" does not exist in the Holy Bible and therefore does not exist – period. There is no such thing as taking the mark of the beast "not on purpose." Jesus said no man can serve two masters, and *no man can be marked by two masters either.*

What God *Seems* to Say About the Mark of the Beast?

> "But it's not so easy, is it, when we're all so new at this and something doesn't jibe with what God seems to say about it?" (*Desecration*, p. 21)

David told Chang that God *seemed* to say something about having the mark of the beast. The Word of God is being made relative here (a New Age tactic), which is necessary so the reader will accept the whole dual-marking demonic lie. The Word of God is clear and not at all ambiguous about the mark of the beast and what the consequences are for anyone who receives this mark (see Rev. 14:10-11).

> "Dr. Ben-Judah's the expert, and you've got him baffled, so I won't pretend to have an answer for you." (*Desecration*, p. 21)

I want to stop and comment on the "Dr. Ben-Judah being the expert" line. The Holy Bible is the only expert that is infallible or without error. What the Holy Bible says stands far above any human authority, and it is the absolute and final authority. Once you read more of David's statements, you will see the authors put question marks into the reader's mind about the authority of the Holy Bible, the very Word of God.

> "But obviously something's not right, and I don't blame you for wanting to find out how God sees you now." (*Desecration*, p. 21)

The Bible tells us how God sees Chang now, and he is damned for all eternity; we must never give more authority to man's explanations than to the inerrant Word of God. This is idolatry, and is causing the falling away of the church.

Later on, the authors used the video taped coverage of Chang's "forced marking" to try to convince the readers to base their beliefs about the mark of the beast on *circumstances* (situation ethics) rather than on the Word of God which will endure forever. David continued,

> "There's no doubt in my mind that nothing can separate you from God and his love, but you're not going to have peace until you know for sure what really happened that morning." (*Desecration*, p. 21)

Notice the implication that even having the mark of the beast cannot separate you from God and his love. Yes it can! What is in David's mind is not the final authority. The final authority about a Christian being marked with Antichrist's mark is written in the Holy Bible, and no matter how hard Satan works through his false teachers, the scriptures cannot be broken.

Chang will not have peace until he finds out the *circumstances* under which he was marked with Satan's mark? Can you see how the authors are trying to get the readers to look at the *circumstances* and opinions of others to determine what is ultimately true regarding a Christian having the mark of the beast? Satan is waiting for Christians to take this bait so they will draw back unto perdition rather than believe unto the saving of their soul (see Heb. 10:39). Only the Holy Bible can be trusted to be a perfect lamp unto our feet and light unto our paths.

Later on in the story we find that yes, the circumstances surrounding Chang being marked with the beast nullified the Bible's stand on the matter in the characters' minds. God forbid that it should have the same effect upon the minds of the readers.

David said:
> "Now, again, let me be clear: "This is not your top priority. "Most important for you is to complete the tasks I listed above and make sure we're all safe and still undetected." (*Desecration*, p. 21)

The writers *again* hammered into the reader's mind that the mark of the beast is no big deal, and that physical matters of survival take precedence over trivial spiritual matters such as a Christian having the mark of Antichrist:

> David transmitted the message, then let Mac read it before they headed off for Mizpe Ramon. Mac nodded.
> "How much time do you give him?" (This question is in reference to how long David thinks Chang will be able to continue in his job position for the Tribulation Force.)
> David shrugged. "Not much, but I don't want to nuke the system because he's on a bathroom break either." (*Desecration*, pp. 22-23)

David, a Christian character, called Chang's internal turmoil over being marked with the beast (which the Bible says results in eternal damnation in smoke and torment) a *"bathroom break"*! This reflects a contempt for things that are sacred, and is an affront to God. A Christian being marked with Satan's mark is an irreversible catastrophe, *not* a non-event as the authors portrayed it in *Desecration*.

The authors went to *great lengths* to discount Chang's spiritual catastrophe so the reader will also.

10

SEX AND THE *LEFT BEHIND* SERIES

Sex is sacred in the sight of God. He created the gift of sex exclusively for the context of the marriage covenant. Satan knows this and because he hates God, he does his utmost to lure people to misuse the gift of sex to their own destruction. It is antichrist to promote anything that has to do with having sex outside of marriage or that promotes lustful thoughts. It is also antichrist to be ashamed of God's holy standards for sexual expression.

The Bible declares,

> Marriage is honourable in all, and the bed undefiled: but whoremongers and adulterers God will judge. (Heb. 13:4)

A whoremonger is a person who engages in the unlawful indulgence of lust, fornication, or adultery. God judges whoremongers severely. Those who commit these sins will have their part in the lake which literally burns with fire and brimstone (see Rev. 21:8). The Lord Jesus Christ will judge all whoremongers.

The authors have treated the sacred subject of sex in an unholy manner in the *Left Behind* series. This particularly grieves the Lord Jesus because He likens the marriage covenant with His own covenant relationship with the church. Just as Jesus loved the church and gave Himself for her, so must the husband love his own wife. Just as the church is subject to Christ in all things, so must the wives be subject to their own husbands (see Eph. 5:24-25). Marriage and sexuality are very sacred and serious in the sight of the true God of the Holy Bible.

The authors sent many anti-biblical messages on the subject of adultery, which have already been covered in Chapter 3. Here, we are going to look at some more ungodly messages they sent on the subject of sex in the book *Tribulation Force*.

Buck Should Not Treat Chloe Like a Sister?

According to the storyline in *Tribulation Force*, it was undesirable, and even insulting, for a Christian older man to treat a younger Christian woman like a sister:

> It didn't make sense. How could he let anything compete with his devotion to God? And yet he couldn't just ignore her, start treating her like a sister. No, he would do the right thing. He would talk to her about it. (*Tribulation Force*, p. 41)

> "He's treating me like a sister, and yet he wants me to drop in and see his place tomorrow." (*Tribulation Force*, p. 77)

According to the narration, if Buck treated Chloe like a sister, he would be ignoring her. The authors put a negative connotation on what the Holy Bible says is God's way for a Christian older man to treat a Christian younger woman:

> "Rebuke not an elder, but entreat him as a father; and the younger men as brethren; the elder women as mothers; the younger as sisters, with all purity." (1 Tim. 5:1-2)

Buck was ten years older than Chloe, and most certainly should have been treating her as a sister with all purity. In Chloe's statement above, she indicated she was upset at being treated like a sister. How would she like to be treated? That is the question signaled to the reader. The implied answer is, "Certainly not like a sister with all purity." The authors chose to make the word "sister" a negative word in the context of a potential romantic interest between an older Christian man and a younger Christian woman.

Christians Can Live Together Out of Wedlock?

Chloe mistakenly thought that Buck was living with a woman he intended to marry, and she was terribly hurt, but would not go to him and speak the truth in love. The ungodly way the authors had her choose to fume about this and not have the forthrightness to confront him with her suspicion is another issue, but I noticed that never once was there any mention of Buck not being truly converted. Those who come to faith in the real Lord Jesus Christ repent; they turn *away* from their sins, and *to* the Lord Jesus Christ. They are turned from darkness to light. The Bible says,

> For ye were sometimes darkness, but now are ye light in the Lord: *walk* as children of light. (Eph. 5:8)

Christians *used* to be in darkness, but now they walk as children of light. If Buck was living with a woman he was not married to, then he was *still* walking in darkness and had not called on the Lord with a pure heart. If Buck was committing the sin of fornication, then he had not believed the gospel in a saving manner and was not following the Lord Jesus Christ.

The thought that Buck was not saved did not cross Rayford's or Chloe's minds. The authors should have made Chloe and Rayford wonder how Buck could possibly be a real Christian and yet have a woman living with him. The reader is left with the notion that he can be a Christian and be sexually immoral too. You can believe in the modern-day "Jesus" and live together with someone out of wedlock, but you cannot have saving faith in the Lord Jesus Christ and live in sexual impurity.

Christian Virgins are Not Cool?

Buck and Chloe had their first "date" by taking a walk late at night after Rayford had gone to bed. This is an example of making *provision* for the sins of the flesh. The authors chose to have this older Christian brother and younger Christian sister act exactly like the world and go off alone together in the middle of the night while her father went to bed. Christians must not put themselves into any situation that would make a way for sexual lusts, which literally war against their souls, to be able to work their way into their hearts and then into their conduct.

While they were talking, the conversation got onto the subject of their past sexual experience. Buck went first in divulging his experiences:

> "One girl, a year ahead of me in grad school, dumped me because I was too slow to make a move on her."

> "No!"
> "Guess I'm a little old-fashioned that way."
> "That's encouraging." (*Tribulation Force*, p. 200)

Being "slow to make a move" is old-fashioned? Notice that the authors did not have Buck say he *was* old-fashioned. They had Buck, as a Christian, think that his past slowness to make a move on a girl *is* old-fashioned.

Chloe went on to ask him to elaborate on his college relationships with girls:

> "You want the truth?"
> "I don't know. Do I?"
> "Depends. Would you rather hear that I have all kinds of experience because I'm such a cool guy, or that I'm a virgin?
> (*Tribulation Force*, p. 200)

The message is plain. Having sexual experience means you are cool, and virgins are not cool. A Christian character is being used to send the message that having sex outside the bonds of marriage is cool, and that being a virgin is anything but cool.

Incredibly, the authors had Buck not know what answer Chloe wanted to hear:

> "You're going to tell me whatever I want to hear?"
> "I'm going to tell you the truth." I just wouldn't mind knowing in advance which you'd rather hear."
> "Experienced or a virgin," Chloe repeated. "That's a no-brainer. Definitely the latter." (*Tribulation Force*, p. 200)

The reader is presented with the idea that a Christian man thinks it is possible that a Christian woman would not want to hear that he has *not* been sexually immoral in his past.

Buck was embarrassed to do so, but he confessed his lack of sexual experience to Chloe:

> "Bingo," Buck said softly, more from embarrassment than from braggadocio."
> "Wow," Chloe said. "That's something to be proud of these days."
> (*Tribulation Force*, p. 200)

Buck went on to say he was grateful, rather than proud, and that his reasons back then were not as pure as they are today:

> "Truth is, people always assumed I got around because I ran in pretty fast circles. But I was backward when it came to stuff like that. Kind of conservative." (*Tribulation Force*, p. 201)

Buck (remember he is supposed to be a Christian character) attributed his non-participation in sexually immoral behavior as *backwardness*. See the word association propaganda technique the authors constantly used in the series? Unmarried virgins are *backward* and *conservative*.

> "You're apologizing."
> "Maybe. I don't mean to be. It's kind of embarrassing to be my age and totally inexperienced. I've always been ahead of my generation in other ways." (*Tribulation Force*, p. 201)

Buck was apologizing because he got to a certain age and still refrained from fornication? Buck was behind his generation because he had not committed fornication (see 1 Cor. 6:18) and sinned against his own body? Buck, *as a Christian*, is embarrassed to be his age and be sexually inexperienced? The message the reader gets from Chloe and Buck's dialogue is that sexual purity is embarrassing, backward, and conservative, especially if you are a man.

Buck Was Ashamed To Admit He Was a Virgin

Chloe pressed Buck to listen to the details of her past experience, or lack of it. Buck did not want to hear it and was embarrassed, but Chloe, showing her feminist tendencies early in the series, insisted on telling him. Before she did, the authors revealed to the reader Buck's thoughts of having admitted to Chloe that he was a virgin:

> Buck was ashamed of himself. It was one thing to admit to a woman that you're a virgin when it seemed to put you in one of the smaller minorities in the world. (*Tribulation Force*, p. 201)

Why did the authors have this *Christian* character think that being sexually pure is something to be ashamed about? Sexual purity is the Lord Jesus Christ's command to His "called out from the world" people. Fornication and uncleanness must not be named even once among saints (see Eph. 5:3). The authors had this Christian character be ashamed of the Word of God:

> "For whosoever shall be ashamed of me and of my words, of him shall the Son of man be ashamed, when he shall come in his own glory, and in his Father's, and of the holy angels." (Luke 9:26)

They also had this character be ashamed that he did not conform to the world. God commands Christians, the called out ones of Jesus Christ, to *not* be conformed to this world, but rather, they must be *renewed* in their minds and "prove what is that good, and acceptable, and perfect, will of God" (Rom. 12:22).

Coarse Jesting

Rayford needed Hattie to encourage Chaim in his faith, so he asked her for a favor. The authors wrote their dialogue about this in a way as to make what is sacred coarse:

> "Could I get you to do me a favor?" Rayford said.
> "Anything."
> "Don't be too quick to say that, Hattie."
> "I mean it. Anything. If it helps you, I'll do it."
> "Well, if you succeed, it helps the cause."
> "Say no more. I'm there."
> "It has to do with Chaim."
> "Isn't he the best?"
> "He's great, Hattie. But he needs something Tsion and I don't seem to be able to give him."
> "Rayford!" He's twice my age!" (*The Mark*, p. 310)

There is no reason to insert coarse jesting into the novel except to desensitize the reader to think that anything goes as a Christian, even coarse jesting. Here is another insertion of coarse jesting into the dialogue of a Christian character:

> "Just tell me if that was Rabbi Tsion Ben-Judah of Israel!"
> "It sounds like you've already named him. What do you need my input for?"
> "So, it *was* him?"
> "You said it. I didn't."
> "But was it?"
> "You want the honest truth, Verna?" That man is my secret lover. I keep him under the bed." (*Nicolae*, p. 346)

Corrupt communications are against the doctrines of the Lord Jesus Christ:

> Let no corrupt communication proceed out of your mouth, but that which is good to the use of edifying, that it may minister grace unto the hearers. (Eph. 4:29)

The Bible Does Not Distinguish Between Homosexuals and Heterosexuals?

After Buck threatened to tell Verna's superiors she was a lesbian, he attempted to witness to her. Buck committed the sin of extortion in order to prevent Verna from alerting Carpathia (Antichrist) to the fact that Buck was not truly a team player. First we have the example presented of a Christian committing the sin of extortion. This sin was justified in the storyline for the same reason the rest of the sins were excused: to save the Christian's life in this world.

Second, blackmail is a work of darkness and a Christian was portrayed as committing this sin for the usual reason. By the way, Homosexuality will be lauded, not condemned, during the tribulation. Satan embraces and promotes everything that perverts the right way of the Lord.

Verna spoke to Buck about what his religion says regarding homosexuals:

> "I mean it, Verna. If you ever want to talk about this stuff, you can come to me."

> "With what your religion says about homosexuals, are you kidding?"
> "My Bible doesn't differentiate between homosexuals and heterosexuals," Buck said. "It may call practicing homosexuals sinners, but it also calls heterosexual sex outside of marriage sinful."
> (*Nicolae*, p. 365)

The writers had a "Christian" character make the politically correct statement that the Bible does not distinguish between homosexuals and heterosexuals. This would include Verna's demeanor, speech, companions, and thought life as long as she did not commit homosexual acts. This is Satan's politically correct lie that is permeating the church today, and those who believe it will be spiritually destroyed. The effeminate (males having feminine qualities untypical of men) and abusers of themselves with mankind shall not inherit the kingdom of God:

> Know ye not that the unrighteous shall not inherit the kingdom of God? Be not deceived: neither fornicators, nor idolaters, nor adulterers, nor effeminate, nor abusers of themselves with mankind, nor thieves, nor covetous, nor drunkards, nor revilers, or extortioners, shall inherit the kingdom of God. (1 Cor. 6:10)

Perversion is Satan's middle name; he loves to pervert God's ways, and this is one obvious example of it. A person with homosexual feelings who has given his life to the Lord Jesus Christ must ask Him for deliverance from the powers of darkness that cause him to behave in an effeminate manner and cause him to desire those of the same sex. Jesus saves to the *uttermost* those who come unto God by Him:

> Wherefore he is able also to save them to the uttermost that come unto God by him, seeing he ever liveth to make intercession for them. (Heb. 7:25)

Cleansing ourselves from all filthiness of flesh and spirit is not only to those who are effeminate but to all fornicators, adulterers, thieves, covetous, drunkards, prideful, etc. Jesus came to deliver us from the power of darkness, not only from the penalty of sin. We must believe His Word and be delivered from the power of darkness in our lives so Satan will have no place in our lives to destroy us when his time of unbridled power comes upon the earth in the tribulation.

Christians Watch Talk Shows?

Buck was rather embarrassed by Chloe's frank disclosure of her (lack of) sexual experience. Chloe ribbed him for not being comfortable talking about such personal issues during their first long conversation, and called him an old codger:

> "C'mon, Buck, you hear this and a lot worse on talk shows every day." (*Tribulation Force,* p. 202)

This message, quickly slipped into the storyline, signals the reader that Christians watch television just like the unbelieving world. Furthermore, Christians watch the *same kinds* of spiritually filthy television shows the world watches. Talk shows at the present time are filled with uncleanness, lewdness, gossip, and all sorts of corruption. Christians who sin against God and partake of this spiritual filth unknowingly invite malevolent spiritual entities into their lives that are looking for the chance to bite "hedge-breaking" Christians. (See Ecc. 10:8) This is one more example of how the characters in the *Left Behind* series walk in the counsel of the ungodly and stand in the way of sinners (see Ps. 1:1) and lead the unwary reader astray.

11

THE ANTICHRIST FOUNDATION OF THE *LEFT BEHIND* SERIES

The "working for the Antichrist" foundation is the starting point for many other antichrist themes promoted in the *Left Behind* series. If the authors did not choose to have the Christian heroes work for the Antichrist, they would not have been able to promote and justify the sinful living that they tried to pass off as Christianity. None of the ungodly examples that were shamefully justified in the storyline are excused in the Holy Bible, which endures forever. Some of them, however, have been justified in the reader's mind, which have set him up to mix up the things of God with the things of Satan.

All of the sins committed by the characters in the series are supposedly to further "the cause." Because serving both the Lord Jesus Christ and serving Antichrist are called "the cause," the reader is even further subverted into confusing the things of Jesus and the things of Satan.

Some themes that stem directly from the "work for the Antichrist" foundation are:

1. The "losing the testimony of Jesus" theme
2. The "go along with the program" theme
3. The "don't reveal the identify of the Antichrist" theme
4. The "save your own life" theme
5. The "hypocrisy and duplicity" theme
6. The "be forced to take the mark of the beast" theme
7. The "submit to being cursed by satanists" theme

8. Last, but certainly not least, the "pledging allegiance to Satan" theme

None of these "against the Lord Jesus Christ" themes could have been foisted upon the reader without the "working for the Antichrist" satanic foundation. Lying, stealing, extortion, covetousness, murder, reviling, malice, guile, hypocrisies, and evil speakings are some of the sins that come to mind as I think of the characters of the *Left Behind* series. These sins are justified in the narration and dialogue because the characters work for the Antichrist, are trying to thwart the Antichrist, have to go and rescue someone from the Antichrist, or are trying to get revenge on the Antichrist.

Some Rules Gone After the Disappearances

Early in the first book in the series, the reader is introduced to the "no more rules" theme. This theme was born from the chaos that ensued from the "disappearances" and actually conditions the reader for the "working for the Antichrist" foundation and all of the examples of wickedness that spring forth from that one.

The "no more rules" theme is simple. The disappearances were a disaster that resulted in death and destruction. Yes, the death and destruction will occur, but not for the reason the authors stated. In times of disaster, rules are abandoned by most people as they do what it takes to survive. But what about the Christian? Enter the "working for the Antichrist" solution of the *Left Behind* series. This solution is hand-picked by Satan for the Christian who wants to save his own life during the tribulation and deceive himself into thinking that he is serving God.

> "You have to admit, when people disappear, some rules go out the window." (*Left Behind*, p. 34)

> "Millions of people disappear into thin air and I should worry about getting written up for riding instead of walking? Later, Steele." (*Left Behind*, p. 44)

Maybe *That's* How God Works

Buck was thinking about falling in love and being married and having children, and he wondered how any of this could fit in with the tribulation. He wondered about how God works. The authors emphasized Buck's thoughts about how God works by italicizing them:

> *Maybe that's how God works,* he thought. *He leads you to logical, or illogical, conclusions.* (*Tribulation Force*, p. 41) [emphasis in the original]

The context of the above quote is not about working for the Antichrist specifically, but it is the way the authors chose to teach the reader about *how God works*. He leads you to logical or illogical conclusions, according to this passage. When the "working for the Antichrist" question comes up, the reader has already been conditioned to think that God can lead you to either logical or illogical conclusions. The real message is that He will lead you to biblical or unbiblical conclusions.

Satan Called and Rayford and Buck Answered

Tribulation Force depicted Nicolae Carpathia (Antichrist) pursuing Rayford and Buck to work in his satanic regime by offering huge financial incentives and by manipulating circumstances behind the scenes. Satan wanted these Christians in his employ to destroy them spiritually, although that is certainly not the way the writers portrayed it.

It is not wrong to have this situation presented in the storyline if the characters responded to it biblically so the reader understands *why* no Christian may knowingly work for a satanist under any circumstances. The authors did not do this, but instead decided to have *God* direct Rayford and Buck to work for the most powerful occultist in the world.

Pastor Advises Rayford and Buck to Consider the Offer Rather Than Flee from Temptation

Bruce moved on to both Rayford's and Buck's new job opportunities. "This may shock all of you, because I have not expressed an opinion yet, but Buck and Rayford, I think both of you should seriously consider accepting these jobs." (*Tribulation Force,* p. 236)

The authors went on to write that the meeting was thrown into an uproar. This is because the reader is in an emotional uproar. Certainly a Christian cannot work for Antichrist and be in a right relationship with God! It simply cannot be possible.

The characters discussed how working for Antichrist would affect their lives. Not once did anyone mention checking the Bible, which is a lamp unto the Christian's feet and a light unto his path. If the characters *did* consult it, the story could not have taken the characters down the broad road of destruction, where they served Satan, supposedly in order to serve God. If the writers had Rayford and Buck consult their *Bibles* about the matter of a Christian being permitted to work for the Antichrist, they would not have been able to have the storyline continue in its very unscriptural manner.

The Bible is so plain that Christians must not give *place* to the devil, which means to not give him any opening or opportunity to work in their lives through sin, ungodly associations, or by "touching the unclean thing" (see Eph. 4:27, 1 Cor. 15:33, 2 Cor. 6:17). The words of the Lord Jesus Christ are easy to understand:

> No man can serve two masters: for either he will hate the one, and love the other; or else he will hold to the one, and despise the other. Ye cannot serve God and mammon. (Matt. 6:24)

Serving two masters is impossible according to the words of Jesus Christ, who cannot lie. It is obvious who is the master of the Tribulation Force. These characters sinned to serve their master. They were actually serving Satan, even though they were depicted as being Christians. Holding the truth in their unrighteousness does not sanctify their actions, no matter how much the writers tried to do this in the storyline.

In real life, Christians are presently deceiving themselves into thinking they can work for companies controlled by Satan's followers and get away with it. They enjoy the income and financial security in their sin, and think God understands that they have no choice but to work for satanically-marked companies, because *that is where the money is*. These compromising Christians will reap what they have sown when the tribulation begins. God will not suddenly give them the desire to turn their backs on the filthy lucre and begin obeying the Lord Jesus Christ. Instead, He will send them strong delusion so they will believe the lie (see 2 Thess. 2:1-12). You must commit to overcome and serve the Lord Jesus Christ without reserve or any compromise whatsoever *today*, and learn to live by faith *today*. If you do this, you will be kept from succumbing to the temptation to save your own life in this world, which will ensure that you will lose it later (see Rev. 3:10). Surviving during the tribulation is *not* about odds, as the *Left Behind* series shamefully and dishonestly teaches. It is about following the Lord Jesus Christ *now* in single-hearted obedience to His voice so we will hear it later when our very lives depend upon it (John 10:37).

A Choice Job Offer?

He was impressed that Rayford did not seem to have his head turned by such a choice job offer but he found himself agreeing with Bruce that Rayford should consider it. (*Tribulation Force,* p. 237)

Buck, the number two hero in the *Left Behind* series, was depicted by the authors as thinking that working for a satanist is a *choice* job offer.

Rationalizations for Working for Antichrist

If God wants you to work for the Antichrist, what better reason could there be? Carpathia predicted that Rayford would soon be flying for him in his employ, and that he would never again be satisfied with a technologically inferior airplane.

> "That may very well be." *But not for that reason,* Rayford thought. *Only if it's what God wants.* (*Tribulation Force*, p. 297) [emphasis in the original]

Bruce hinted that the men should think about accepting Antichrist's job offers, but Chloe was certain that both her father and Buck should work for Antichrist. In fact, she seemed to lead the meeting and countered the objections the men had to this proposition. (Chloe's feminist tendencies continued throughout the series.)

> "I think you should both take the jobs." (*Tribulation Force*, p. 238)
>
> "I'm not discounting the horror you went through, Buck. But without someone on the inside, Carpathia is going to deceive everyone." (*Tribulation Force*, p. 238)
>
> Buck was not convinced. "I'd have to sell out every journalistic principle I have."
> "And those are more sacred than your responsibilities to your brothers and sisters in Christ?" (*Tribulation Force*, p. 239)

Chloe's rationalization for Rayford and Buck working for the leader of the New Global Order was that if there were no Christians posing as satanists, then everyone would be deceived. The authors did not initially reveal to the reader that the leader of the New World Order will be a person who knowingly worships Satan, and they never revealed that all the employees in high levels of his organization will be satanists.

The whole point of the tribulation is *not* for God to extend his mercy to people who have refused to be saved as the *Left Behind* series outrageously teaches. It will really be a time when God finally will allow the sinful world to openly serve Satan without being restrained in any way by the Holy Spirit.

> He who now letteth will let, until he be taken out of the way.
> (2 Thess. 2:7)

Working for Antichrist was even made out to be Buck's responsibility to his brothers and sisters in Christ. What incredible manipulation on the part of the authors. God will never have a

Christian violate His Word. Quite conveniently, the authors never had the characters bring up God's immutable Word, but instead, had the group pray.

Working for the Antichrist was God's Answer to Prayer?

Do you remember the "maybe that's how God works" quote cited earlier that was in reference to Buck's thoughts about love, marriage, and having children? The authors had Buck think that God will lead a Christian to logical or illogical conclusions. The "God working logically or illogically" mini-theme was *repeated* while the four Tribulation Force members (Bruce, Rayford, Buck, and Chloe) knelt to pray to seek God's will about working for Antichrist's regime. The "logical or illogical" mini-theme was repeated because the reader needed some extra mind manipulation about God's supposed methods in order to accept the notion that God would have one of His called-out ones called back into a life of sin working for the Antichrist.

> As Rayford knelt there, he realized he needed to surrender his will to God – again. Apparently this would be a daily thing, giving up the logical, the personal, the tightfisted, closely held stuff." (*Tribulation Force*, p. 240)

> Rayford knelt there in front of his chair, his hands covering his face, praying silently. Whatever God wanted was what he wanted, even if it made no sense from a human standpoint. (*Tribulation Force*, p. 240)

Extra Manipulation to Help the Reader Accept that Working for the Antichrist is God's Will

> He had never felt so vividly the presence of God. So this was the feeling of dwelling on holy ground, what Moses must have felt when God told him to remove his shoes. Rayford wished he could sink lower into the carpet, could cut a hole in the floor and hide from the purity and infinite power of God. (*Tribulation Force*, p. 241)

Rayford was depicted as being able to sense the very presence of God, to the point of wanting to hide from his presence and purity. While this was going on, Rayford was giving up the *logical* things; he wanted what God wanted even if it made no sense from a human standpoint. The Bible was completely left out, and a presence came into the room, seemingly approving of the way Rayford and Buck were headed. The way they were headed was in complete opposition to the Holy Bible, so who really was that presence? He was someone who made himself out to be an angel of light. He was not the true Light who is Jesus Christ, because he approved what was against the Word of God.

> Satan himself is transformed into an angel of light. (2 Cor. 11:14)

The presence that *seemed* so holy and pure was *not* the God of the Bible; it was the god of this world counterfeiting the Most High God. This unclean spirit had the opportunity or "place" to give a counterfeit sense of peace to these Christians who did not prove what is acceptable to the Lord by searching the scriptures. Instead, they leaned unto their own understanding and did not acknowledge God's Word so he could use it to direct their paths.

Working For Antichrist Equals Living an Antichrist Life

What better way to promote an antichrist agenda than to have the characters work for Antichrist and thus be "forced" to engage in a sinful lifestyle which is the opposite of how *true* Christians endure tribulation, which is by patience and faith (2 Thess. 1:4).

The Bible teaches that saints must live godly during tribulation, yet the *Left Behind* series teaches ungodliness during tribulation. Here are some examples of how God's people are to walk in the Spirit and overcome, not *be* overcome: David the psalmist wrote,

> They had almost consumed me upon earth; but I forsook not thy precepts. (Ps. 119:87)

> Trouble and anguish have taken hold on me: yet thy commandments are my delights. (Ps. 119:143)

> Many are my persecutors and mine enemies; yet do I not decline
> from thy testimonies. (Ps. 119:157)

The *real* God of the Holy Bible requires us to exercise the same diligence we had at the beginning so we will have full assurance of the hope of salvation unto the end. God will *not* allow us to be slothful (not diligent to obey) like the *Left Behind* series characters. Just like the people of faith in times past, we will inherit the promises through faith and patience (see Heb. 6:11-12).

"God" Led Rayford to Serve Antichrist

Even though the Most High God would never violate His own Word and lead any Christian to unite himself with known satanists, the authors repeatedly made the point that God led Rayford to work for Antichrist. The "God" who lead Rayford to work for Antichrist is not the Lord of Hosts of the Bible, because he is against the teachings of the Bible, and is therefore really Satan. The authors had Rayford willing to work for Antichrist "only if it's what God wants."

It would almost be understandable if the writers would have had the *Left Behind* series depict Christians as being deceived into uniting with Antichrist in order to slow him down in his plans of destruction. They could then have shown the horrible consequences the characters reaped because they disobeyed God and gave place to the devil. But they did not use the "working for the Antichrist" theme to teach the consequences of disobedience to God. Instead, they made *God* the sinner by having Rayford yoke together with the top-level satanist in the world. They repeatedly try to get the reader to think that the God of the Bible is the antichrist "God" they depict in their book series.

The "God led Rayford to work for Antichrist" theme is repeated in the books so the reader will be convinced of this unbiblical "fact." The real God, who is holy, will never lead Christians to work for satanists no matter how it is rationalized.

> How proud Irene would have been of this moment, when he had
> the top job in the flying world. But to him it meant little, though he

felt in his spirit that he was doing what God had led him to do. (*Tribulation Force*, p. 310)

Biblical Proof the Real God Did Not Lead Rayford to Work for Antichrist

At least not God, the Most High. God's commands for how his children are to serve their employers completely prohibit a Christian from being able to work for Antichrist.

> Servants, be obedient to them that are your masters according to the flesh, with fear and trembling, in singleness of your heart, as unto Christ; Not with eye-service, as menpleasers; but as the servants of Christ, doing the will of God from the heart; with good will doing service, as to the Lord, and not to men. (Eph. 6:5-8)

Let us prove all things and test whether or not it was the God of the Holy Bible who led Rayford and Buck to serve in Antichrist's employ. These men went into the job in disobedience to the above-mentioned Bible verse.

1. They went in knowing they would serve Antichrist outwardly ("menpleasers") but inwardly they would be subversive and do their best to work *against* the man who was paying them to carry out his orders.

2. Their exhorbitant pay was really stolen goods because they purposely tried not to earn it, but merely to *look* like they worked for it

3. They chose to commit the daily sins of lying, hypocrisy and guile in order to work for Antichrist, which is the opposite of serving him with a single heart. They could not serve Antichrist and do service to the Lord God of the Bible because in order to serve Antichrist, they had to cast *off* the armor of light and put on the works of darkness (see Rom. 13:12).

Antichrist, however, would definitely want to yoke Christians with himself so that Satan would have a broken hedge with which he could "bite" the Christian whenever he pleased.

The Counterfeit "Presence" Gave Bruce and Chloe a Direct Leading in Favor of the Antichrist

> At ten o'clock, when they were getting ready to leave, Buck turned to Rayford. "As wonderful as that prayer time was, I didn't get any direct leading about what to do."
> "Me either."
> "You must be the only two." Bruce glanced at Chloe, and she nodded. "It's pretty clear to us what you should do." (*Tribulation Force*, pp. 242-43)

Satan can make himself appear as an angel of light. Any presence, no matter how holy it may appear, is not the God of the Holy Bible if it affirms what God's Word opposes. God's Word affirms that:

> No man can serve two masters: for either he will hate the one, and love the other; or else he will hold to the one, and despise the other. Ye cannot serve God and mammon. (Matt. 6:24)

The "God" who made His leading known to Bruce and Chloe was leading contrary to the Holy Scriptures. This seemingly holy presence was none other than Satan.

Rationalizing Away Rayford's Accountability to God

> Rayford knew he was not responsible for what Nicolae Carpathia meted out against his enemies. The terrible dark judgement on the earth rendered by this evil man would not stop if Rayford merely quit his job. (*Nicolae*, p. 119)

Rayford *was* responsible for what Nicolae was meting out upon his enemies. He was the "devil's own pilot" (*Nicolae*, p. 95) and he was helping the devil kill his enemies, who happened to be Rayford's brethren. This character was depicted as rationalizing his sins so he could continue to serve Satan while tricking himself into thinking he was serving God.

No, the cruelty that Nicolae was perpetrating on Christians would not stop if Rayford quit his job, but Rayford would still be held accountable for the people harmed or killed by his willingness to be Antichrist's accomplice in the guise of service to God.

> He didn't need the job, didn't want the job, didn't ask for the job. Somehow, he knew that God had placed him there. (*Nicolae*, p. 119)

Do you remember how Rayford "knew" that God had placed him in daily contact with occultists? He sensed the presence of "God" while he prayed, and other Christians were directly led by this "God" that he should work for the man of sin.

> Rayford shrugged. He wasn't sure why God had put him in this position, but until he felt led to leave it, he would hang in. (*Soul Harvest*, p. 88)

Hypocrisy: Devilish Wisdom

The writers portrayed the Christian characters in the *Left Behind* series doing the very same thing satanists do in real life. Satanists infiltrate Christian ministries and *pose* as believers so as to gain trust and then positions of power. This is done for the purpose of subverting them. The authors had the Christian characters behave like Satan's followers. They lied continuously just like Satan's agents do in serving the father of liars.

The *Left Behind* series portrayed the members of the Tribulation Force using cunning and hypocrisy in order to serve "God". The characters who did this were represented as being full of wit and cleverness. But this wisdom is devilish:

> But this wisdom descendeth not from above, but is earthly, sensual, devilish. (James 3:14)

The wisdom that comes from God is without hypocrisy:

> But the wisdom that is from above is first pure, then peaceable, gentle, *and* easy to be intreated, full of mercy and good fruits, without partiality, and without hypocrisy. (James 3:17)

This is only one example of "speaking lies in hypocrisy," which the Bible says will cause you to have your conscience seared with a hot iron (see 1 Tim. 4:2).

After Chang received his forced marking, Walter Moon and Mr. Wong brought him to David Hassid to be interviewed. Walter Moon affirmed the lordship of Antichrist, and David, speaking a lie in hypocrisy, followed suit:

> Walter Moon said, "He is risen."
> Mr. Wong and David responded, "He is risen indeed."
> (*The Mark*, p. 346)

The authors even had David "play act" and incriminate a fellow Christian for a crime he did not commit so he would not "jeopardize his position" working for Antichrist:

> "The camera doesn't lie," Leon said. "We have our assassin, don't we?" Much as he wanted to come up with some other explanation for what was clear, David would jeopardize his position if he proved illogical. He nodded. "We sure do." (*The Indwelling*, p. xiii)

Jesus said hypocrites have a place, and it is a place of weeping and gnashing of teeth:

> And shall cut him asunder, and appoint *him* his portion with the hypocrites: there shall be weeping and gnashing of teeth. (Matt. 24:51)

Bible Christians (not the *Left Behind* kind) must lay aside all malice, guile, and hypocrisies, and envies and all evil speakings (see 2 Pet. 1:1). Yes, even during the tribulation. The time in history does not change the fact that Christians are to manifest the truth, and be "flesh-and-blood epistles, living messages that can be read by everyone."[1]

One More Way to Die?

The reader learns from Bruce Barnes that during the tribulation, the Christian has one more way to die than the unbeliever:

> "Everyone else is in danger of death, too. The only difference is, we have one more way to die than they do."
> "As martyrs."
> "Right." (*Left Behind,* p. 419)

Christians *do* have another way to die, but it is not just physically dying as taught in the *Left Behind* series. Christians *die to themselves* as Jesus Christ lives in them in the person of the Holy Spirit. They die to self daily as they live unto the Lord Jesus Christ.

The authors did *not* have Bruce explain that Christians have another way to *live*, and that this kind of living is by the faith of the Son of God, who loved him and gave Himself for him (see Gal. 2:20).

Satan's Servants Know Who the Christians Are

Satanists know who a Christian is on sight. A Christian wearing a disguise will not keep a satanist from knowing he belongs to Jesus Christ. This is because satanists have in their bodies demons that they have invited into their lives and who communicate with them constantly. Demons knew who Jesus Christ was when he walked the earth:

> And cried with a loud voice, and said, What have I to do with thee, Jesus, thou Son of the most high God? I adjure thee by God, that thou torment me not. (Mark 5:7)

> And unclean spirits, when they saw him, fell down before him, and cried, saying, Thou art the Son of God. (Mark 3:11)

Satanists know which Christians separate themselves unto God and thus are strong, and which ones are weak and give place to the devil. They do not need to be told by the Christian himself. Their demons tell them immediately, and give instructions so they will know how to hurt the sinning Christian who is giving them "place." The Bible says "Neither give place to the devil." There is a good reason for that, because place can indeed be given (see Eph. 4:27).

Christians Submitting Themselves to Satanists

The authors gave some examples of David actually giving place to the devil by allowing the False Prophet to lay hands on him twice and impart demons to him. Of course the authors had nothing happen to David as a result of his disobedience to God's Word, but in real life, he would have had demons imparted to him:

> Lay hands suddenly on no man, neither be partaker of other men's sins: keep thyself pure. (1 Tim. 5:22)

The False Prophet and two other directors summoned David to meet with them so they could query him about his impressions about Carpathia's murderer on video:

> *I will not kneel*, David vowed. *I will not worship or kiss his hand. Lord, protect me.* (*The Indwelling*, p. 206) [emphasis in the original]

The reader sees this passage in italics and then watches the story closely to see if David kneels, worships, or kisses the False Prophet's hand. This was a ploy to have the reader accept what David actually *did* do, which was submit to being cursed by the highest-level satanist alive in the world at the time. The way the authors described Leon's dealings with David is accurate in that it is one of the ways satanists curse people:

> Leon approached him, and David froze. The supreme commander took David's face in his fleshy hands and looked deep into his eyes. David fought the urge to look away, praying all the while that he would do the right thing and hoping that Annie would continue to pray too. Like Nicolae, here was a man with clear mind control over unbelievers. (*The Indwelling*, p. 208)

Immediately the idea is presented that David should not look away, and that he was doing the right thing. This is completely false.

He should have looked away, and no, he was not doing the right thing. He was giving place to the devil. Why did the authors present a Christian submitting himself to a satanist to be cursed? And why did they present the idea that he was doing the right thing in the sight of God? The authors also gave the reader the impression that only *unbelievers* can have their minds controlled by a person with such high-ranking demons. Not content to have a Christian give such blatant place to the devil once, the writers had David submit to Leon's demonic touch a second time:

> To his disgust, David had to submit a second time to Leon's hands on his face. "Well?" Leon said, peering at him. "Is there any doubt?"
> (*The Indwelling*, p. 209)

David, depicted as being completely unaffected by the accursed laying on of hands, bore false witness against his Christian brother to appease the False Prophet:

> "We sure do," he managed. "Steele must pay." (*The Indwelling*, p 210)

What an evil snare! Christians can and do get demons imparted to them by the laying on of hands, and it does not happen only in books. It happens in churches all the time as infiltrating occultists come up and lay hands suddenly on any Christian they so desire. Because the Word of God is willfully violated, Christians do receive the demons that are imparted to them.

The Authors Had "Christian" Characters in Job Positions *Only* Given to Satanists

Antichrist offered Buck a position (which Buck later accepted) only a *follower of Satan* would be permitted to have during the tribulation:

> "The bottom line here is that I am going to purchase major media, and I want you to be a part of it."
> "Part of what?"
> "Part of the management team. I will become sole owner of the great newspapers of the world, the television networks, the wire services. You may run for me any one of those you wish."
> (*Tribulation Force,* p. 126)

David Hassid definitely had a position only a high-level satanist would be granted:

> David Hassid, mid-twenties; high-level director for the GC; New Babylon. (*The Mark,* p. viii)

This character also went along with Satan's program all for the purpose of serving the cause. "Going along with the program" and saying Antichrist has risen indeed is serving Satan, no matter what a person says he believes.

Buck's *One* Act of Resistance to Antichrist

The Tribulation Force's mission was to go on the offensive against Antichrist, and subvert him in his plans of destruction during the tribulation. Bruce Barnes explained:

> "When it becomes obvious who the Antichrist is, the false prophet, the evil, counterfeit religion, we'll have to oppose them, speak out against them. We would be targeted. Christians content to hide in basements with their Bibles might escape everything but earthquakes and wars, but we will be vulnerable to everything." (*Left Behind,* p. 420)

The authors want the readers to think that ordinary Christians will be safe hiding in their basements. This is untrue and is setting

Christians up to think they will not be hunted down with the use of sophisticated technology for being dissidents during the New World Order regime. Planes and helicopters have sensitive radar that can detect the body heat of human beings as they fly over houses. God is able to protect and override this, but basements and "safehouses" will not keep Christians safe unless they are walking in a covenant relationship with God.

Bruce explained to Buck the mission of the Tribulation Force.

> "It's a band of serious-minded people who will boldly oppose the Antichrist." (*Left Behind*, p. 428)

Later on, in the Tribulation Force, the authors inserted a print subliminal that contradicts Bruce's stated goals of the Tribulation Force.

> Buck's one act of resistance to Carpathia was to ignore the rumors of Fitzhugh plotting with the militia to oppose the Global Community regime by force. (*Tribulation Force*, p. 405)

Buck resisted Carpathia with *one* act? See the hidden message of "go along with the program" By the way, the authors want the reader to think the president of the United States of America will go against the regime of the New World Order. This is totally inaccurate because the government of the United States of America is *leading* the world into the New World Order.

Survival is *Not* About Odds

Getting the reader to think that survival will be a matter of odds during the tribulation was paramount to the success of the antichrist foundation of the *Left Behind* series. Sinning in order to survive would not be easily believed by the reader unless he thought that God would not protect His own obedient children and survival would be nothing but a matter of odds:

> The odds are, only one of the four members of the Tribulation Force will survive the next seven years. (*Tribulation Force*, p. x)

He knew the odds. Each had only a one in four chance of surviving until the Glorious Appearing. (*The Indwelling,* p. 42)

"None of us are likely to make it to the Glorious Appearing, but that's been my goal since day one. What are the odds now?" Mac shook his head. (*Soul Harvest,* p. 341)

Christians Have No More Protection Than the Ungodly?

And if Bruce Barnes could be believed, there was no more protection for believers now, during this period, than there was for anyone else. (*Left Behind,* p. 441)

The only way this statement would come true is if the Christian reader believes the antichrist messages in the *Left Behind* book series and loses patience and the faith of Jesus and thus puts himself outside of the protection of God. Jesus prayed that His disciples (who will be hated by the world because they keep his works) would not be taken out of this world, but that they would be kept from the evil (see John 17:14-15). Jesus wants His people to be kept from evil. *This* is the will of the Lord Jesus Christ.

He commands Christians to be not conformed to this world, but rather to be transformed by the renewing of their minds. Christians must not be deceived into traveling the broad road while they think they are trusting Jesus, who is the God of the narrow way.

Protection is available to Christians during the tribulation the same way it is available today. Jesus wants to keep you from evil – especially spiritual evil. Some Christians will die during the tribulation, but not all will die and survival certainly is not a matter of odds the way the *Left Behind* series makes it out to be. Whether or not the Lord decides to physically protect His people during this time depends upon Him of course, but those He chooses to protect must enter into an unconditional covenant of obedience with the Lord Jesus.

Shadrach, Meshach, and Abednego were examples of having an unconditional covenant of obedience to the Lord Most High. They did not know if He would preserve their physical lives, but they knew he could and he chose to do this to bring honor and glory to His name.

We have the same God today; the question is, will we serve Him with single-eyed devotion the way they did? He is capable of preserving us through the fires of the tribulation and keeping us alive unto His coming. It is cruelly manipulative to tell Christians that during the time of the tribulation there is no more protection for Christians than there is for those outside the family of God.

Are you willing to obey Jesus and be not of the world, even as he is not of this world? If you are, you can receive the answer to Jesus' prayer of being spiritually protected from being deceived into yoking together with Satan to save your own life during the tribulation. It is possible that God would covenant with you to protect you physically as well and preserve you until the Glorious Appearing. You must fast and pray and ask the Lord what He would have you do as you turn your life over to him completely. You may lose all your friends, your family, and your church if they are not repenting right along with you, but whatever it costs, it will be worth it all as Jesus leads you in the paths of righteousness for His name's sake.

12

MERGING WITH THE KINGDOM OF ANTICHRIST

No Christian would be able to work for Antichrist's regime without yielding himself to be a servant of unrighteousness unto sin. Because the whole purpose of Antichrist's regime is to serve Satan in opposition to God, all employees in his regime will carry out his unrighteous schemes. Any Christian serving Antichrist, even for the reason of trying to subvert him, would not be under the grace of God because those under the dominion of sin are not under grace:

> For sin shall not have dominion over you: for ye are not under the law, but under grace. (Rom. 6:14)

Whoever a Christian yields himself to obey is his master:

> Know ye not, that to whom ye yield yourselves servants to obey, his servants ye are to whom ye obey; whether of sin unto death, or of obedience unto righteousness? (Rom. 6:16)

The Christians in the *Left Behind* series yielded themselves in service to Antichrist, and they used their master's tools – sin – in order to do him service. Yes, through the sin of hypocrisy and duplicity they supposedly served God by subverting Antichrist. This is not acceptable service unto God, and even in their subversions they were serving Satan. God commands that Christians present their bodies to Him as holy, living sacrifices:

> I beseech you therefore, brethren, by the mercies of God, that ye present your bodies a living sacrifice, holy, acceptable unto God, *which is* your reasonable service. (Rom. 12:1)

The real God will not accept the service of a Christian who "sins in order to serve" as the authors had the Christians in the *Left Behind* series do as a daily lifestyle.

> "No man can serve two masters: for either he will hate the one, and love the other; or else he will hold to the one, and despise the other. Ye cannot serve God and mammon." (Matt. 6:24)

The premise of the "working for Antichrist" theme is against the doctrines of Jesus Christ. Jesus said you cannot serve two masters, or two kingdoms, and the authors presented Christians whose "God" told them to serve both. They could not, and you will see which master they chose. It was not Jesus.

Christianity Depicted as a Rebellion

> But with his secret conversion, Mac had become a mole, subversive, part of the rebellion. A lifetime of military training, self-discipline, chain of command, all-for-one-and-one-for-all thinking was now conflicted. Having reached the pinnacle as a career big-plane pilot, he now used every trick and wile he had ever learned to serve the cause of God. (*Assassins*, p. 66)

In keeping with the antichrist agenda of the *Left Behind* series, the authors communicated that with his conversion, Mac became part of the rebellion. This is a print subliminal. Christianity is being equated with being the rebellion. This is not the dialogue of the GC, who are Satan's followers who will be implementing The Plan to bring in Lucifer's New World Order. This is the author's narration that is linking being a Christian with being part of the rebellion. The message to the reader is that Christianity is part of the rebellion. The only people who think this are Satan's agents who cannot wait to bring in their Hour of Dark Power (the New Age and New Global Order) so they can put down this rebellion once and for all.

Tricks and Wiles to Serve God?

A Christian that has been taught the truth of the Jesus of the Bible repents of deceitfulness:

> If so be that ye have heard him, and have been taught of him, the truth is in Jesus: That ye put off concerning the former conversation the old man, which is corrupt according to the deceitful lusts; And be renewed in the spirit of your mind; and that ye put on the new man, which after God is created in righteousness and true holiness.
> Eph. 4:21-24

Real Christians do not serve God using deception, which is Satan's number one tool. The authors ignored this Bible fundamental and depicted Mac, a new Christian, using Satan's tools to serve God:

> Having reached the pinnacle as a career big-plane pilot, he now used every trick and wile he had ever learned to serve the cause of God. (*Assassins* p. 66)

Christians use *tricks* and *wiles* to serve God? The authors used their word association technique to connect words that apply to the devil, and made them apply to God. The result is that God and the devil become connected by the use of a well-known verse. The New Living Translation uses the word *tricks* and the King James Bible uses the word *wiles* in the same verse that speaks of the devil's tools:

> "Put on all of God's armor so that you will be able to stand firm against all strategies and tricks of the Devil." New Living Translation (Eph. 6:11)
> "Put on the whole armour of God, that ye may be able to stand against the wiles of the devil." King James Bible. (Eph. 6:11)

Tricks and wiles are tools of the devil, but the authors want you to think they are tools of the Christian.

Embezzlement For Jesus Sake?

Since serving "God" by sinning in service to Antichrist is what the *Left Behind* series is based on, sin is usually "sanctified" in the storyline by clever rationalizations.

After the destruction of Washington and the resulting chaos, Buck determined he needed a new vehicle:

> "I need a new car," he said. "Something tells me it's going to be our only chance to survive." (*Nicolae*, p. 12)

Buck made a fortune working for Antichrist, but instead of spending his own ill-gotten money, he charged a Range Rover that cost almost one hundred thousand dollars to Antichrist's account. This sin of embezzlement was justified in the storyline as a way to serve God, thus maligning the character of the Most High:

> "Do you feel like you just spent the Devil's money?" Chloe asked Buck as he carefully pulled the beautiful, new, earth-toned Range Rover out of the dealership and into traffic.
> "I know I did," Buck said. "And the Antichrist has never invested a better dollar for the cause of God."
> "You consider spending almost a hundred thousand dollars on a toy like this an investment in our cause?" (*Nicolae*, p. 24)

Buck went on to describe the features of the vehicle purchased with stolen money. Chloe's rhetorical question did the job. The implied answer is, "Yes."

Sinning in Order to Fight the Antichrist

> Buck lowered the back seat and Leah slid the whole bed in. "You're stealing that?" he said.
> "I put more in my purse than the bed's worth," she said. "You want to debate ethics or fight the GC?" (*Assassins*, p. 45)

Stealing, lying, extorting, embezzling, murdering, and all manner of sin is justified in the *Left Behind* series as being ways for the saints of God to overcome the beast. This is antichrist because it contradicts the teachings of Jesus Christ. The true Christian faith overcomes the world. It is *not* overcome by the world like the characters in the *Left Behind* series are. Jesus said an overcomer is one who keeps his works unto the end (see Rev. 2:26), not someone who keeps Satan's works unto the end.

The following is yet another example to the reader that Christians may be lawless during the tribulation:

> "Leah, Rayford said carefully, "we're talking about the supernatural, good and evil, the battle of the ages. There are no rules, at least not human ones." (*Assassins*, p. 116)

Tell Satan's Agents What they Want to Hear

Mac sent a message to the newest Christian who was also about to step onto the broad road of destruction by working for Satan's top man himself:

> "Personnel will ask straight out about your loyalty to the cause, to the Global Community, to the potentate. Remember, you are a frontline warrior. Tell them what they want to hear." (*Assassins*, p. 67)

The psychologically manipulative writing does not let up in the *Left Behind* series. The message is that if you are a frontline warrior for Jesus Christ you will answer "Yes" to questions designed to determine your loyalty to the cause (Satan), your loyalty to the Global Community (New World Order), and your loyalty to the potentate (Antichrist). This is a wily setup for when they later on have Chang actually answer questions where he verbally answers "Yes" to questions such as "Are you loyal to the supreme potentate?"

Frontline warriors tell Antichrist's employees what they want to hear? Frontline warriors who state they are loyal to Satan, the New World Order, and Antichrist are *not* Christians. They serve Antichrist. The God of the *Left Behind* series is against the doctrines of the Lord Jesus Christ. The God of the *Left Behind* series is Satan.

Denying Jesus Christ Before Men

How do you get masses of Christians to think that during the coming tribulation their Heavenly Father will look the other way if they deny Jesus Christ to save their own life? You put this message in a fictional story and entertain the reader to his spiritual death, all the while using the propaganda technique of rationalization:

> Rationalization. Individuals or groups may use favorable generalities to rationalize questionable acts or beliefs. Vague and pleasant phrases are often used to justify such actions or beliefs.[1]

Annie related that David saw the "mark of the believer" on her forehead and summoned her to his office:

> "As soon as I got in there and the door was shut, he said, 'You're a believer!'"
> "I was scared to death. I said, 'No, I – a believer in what?'"
> "He said, 'Don't deny it! I can see it on your face!'"
> He had to be fishing, so I denied it again. He said, 'You deny Jesus one more time, you're going to be just like Peter. Watch out for a rooster.'
> "I had no idea what he was talking about. I couldn't have told you that Peter was a disciple, let alone that he had denied Christ. David had guessed my secret, mentioned someone named Peter, and was jabbering about a rooster. Still, I couldn't help myself. I said, 'I'm not denying Jesus.'"
> "He said, what do you call it?"
> "I said, 'Fearing for my life.'"
> "He said, 'Welcome to the club. I'm a believer too.'"
> (*Assassins*, p. 38-39)

David's favorable response to Annie's reprehensible act of denying Jesus Christ was to say, "Welcome to the club. I'm a believer too." David's answer indicates that everyone denies Jesus when they are afraid of dying for the testimony of Christ.

The pleasant phrase David used to justify Annie's action was to joke about watching out for a rooster. "Loosen up, Christian, denying Jesus Christ is to be expected when you fear for your life." This is every inch propaganda to get the Christian to "go along with the program" in serving Antichrist by losing the testimony of Jesus."

Pretending to Pray to Antichrist

Ming and Chang, who were both Christians of the "denying Christ kind," accompanied their parents, who were not believers, to pay respects to Nicolae Carpathia, (Antichrist) after his death. The False Prophet, Leon Fortunato, invited the crowd to worship the image of Antichrist. This invitation to worship came right after three of the ten potentates were incinerated where they sat for "glaring stonily" when they were supposed to be worshipping the Antichrist's image:

> "You need not fear your lord god," he said, as the applause continued. What you have witnessed here shall never befall you if you love Nicolae with the love that brought you here to honor his memory. Now before the interment, once everyone has had a chance to pay last respects, I invite you to come and worship. Come and worship. Worship your god, your dead yet living king." (*The Indwelling*, p. 351)

This was definitely a test like the one Shadrach, Meshach, and Abednego were given, and this has not escaped the reader's notice. What should a Christian do when he is expected to honor the beast and his image?

> Ming and Chang sat with hands covering their eyes, appearing to pray. To anyone else, it might appear they were praying to the new god of the world, but David knew. (*The Indwelling*, p. 353)

According to this example, the answer is to "go along with the program" like Ming and Chang did. They *pretended* to worship the image of the beast. This is literally denying the Lord Jesus Christ before men in action, and is antichrist to the core. The Bible teaches that Christians will overcome him by the blood of the Lamb, by the word of their testimony, and by *not loving their lives* unto the death. Ming and Chang loved their own lives in this world and were overcome by the beast by pretending to worship him and thereby blaspheming Jesus Christ. If the reader accepts this diabolical example, he will lose his own soul.

Acknowledging Antichrist as Lord

Incredibly, The authors depicted Christians in the series confessing with their lips that Antichrist is the risen Lord. Viv Ivins wanted to speak with David. The authors narrated David's thoughts about how the Christians who worked for Antichrist would respond to the salutation that is a requirement for all his employees:

> He was so glad she had not begun with the obligatory "He is risen," which he and Mac and Abdullah and Hannah had decided they would respond to with "He is risen indeed," privately knowing they were referring to Christ. (*The Mark*, p. 164)

Privately knowing they were referring to Jesus Christ while publicly confessing Antichrist is denying Jesus Christ before men. Later on, in *Desecration,* The authors had Chang confess Antichrist before men while privately believing in Jesus. These are dangerous hell-sending examples that the reader must reject outright in the name of Jesus Christ.

Here is another example along the same line. David verbally agreed with Viv Ivins' statement about whom they (both) worship:

> "There's no Enigma Babylon One World Faith anymore, because there's no enigma. We know whom to worship now, don't we, Mr. Hassid?"
> "We sure do, he said. (*The Mark*, p. 174)

Viv Ivin's rhetorical question was really a statement in disguise. Her implied statement was: "We know whom we worship." David agreed with the implication of "We worship Antichrist."

Final Step: The Luciferic Initiation

Chang was a member of the Tribulation Force, which was a group of people supposedly serving Jesus Christ in the storyline. In reality, they served the God of Forces because they followed him in serving sin and seared their consciences with a hot iron as they outwardly honored him as their Lord. Chang worked in Antichrist's palace and co-mingled with Luciferians on a daily basis.

One day, a decision was made to interview each member of the staff with polygraph software to determine which person in the palace was not a loyal worker in the administration of Satan's kingdom on earth. Chang, in service to "God" wanted to be certain he passed this test and proved his loyalty to Satan's cause.

The authors had this character think that if the wording to the questions he was given was not specific enough, then he could pass the sophisticated polygraph and fool Satan's workers into thinking he was truly one of them. This is spiritually perverted that they depicted a Christian trying so hard to be taken as Satan's follower but then the title, *Desecration,* is not really about the desecration of a temple made with hands. God does not reside in a physical building anymore. *Desecration* is really about the desecration of the temple of the Holy Spirit – the Christian.

The reader is now being made privy to Chang's thoughts before he took the questions that would prove he was truly loyal to Satan:

> Lars handed him a lapel microphone. "Put this on."
> Chang applied it to his shirt, praying silently. The key, he knew, was how the questions were worded. In his mind, a mole was an animal; he was a human being. If the questions were too specific and unequivocal, he'd be in trouble. (*Desecration*, p. 317-18)

Chang was given some initial neutral "test" questions such as "Is the sky blue?" Then the questions to prove his loyalty to Satan in the Kingdom of Antichrist began:

> "Are you loyal to the supreme potentate?" (*Desecration*, p. 322)

This phrase was specific because the *meaning* of the phrase was known to the questioner, to Chang, and most importantly, to the reader. Chang and his interrogator knew that the question was specifically asked to determine if he was truly loyal to Antichrist, Satan's head representative in the New Global Order.

Chang was at a moment of choosing between Jesus and eternal life, and Satan and eternal death. He chose Satan, just as he did earlier when he would not admit he belonged to Jesus Christ even when his father made it clear to him that he was to receive the mark of the beast. But the authors want the reader to accept his rationalization for denying Jesus Christ:

> Chang closed his eyes and reminded himself that Jesus Christ was the only person who fit that description.
> "Yes," he said. (*Desecration*, p. 322)

Even in this rationalization for his sin there is a hidden antichrist statement. Jesus Christ is not the supreme potentate. He is the ONLY potentate:

> Which in his times he shall shew, who is the blessed and only Potentate, the King of Kings, and Lord of lords; Who only hath immortality, dwelling in the light which no man can approach unto; whom no man hath seen, nor can see: to whom be honour and power everlasting. 1 Tim. 15,16

Chang was even asked if the "supreme potentate" (Antichrist's title in the series) had risen from the dead and was the living lord:

> "Is the supreme potentate risen from the dead and the living lord?"
> "Yes." (*Desecration*, p. 322)

Chang actually took the Luciferic Initiation. The Luciferic Initiation is "a submission to Lucifer as the leading divinity representing the Logos"[2] Everyone must take the Luciferic Initiation to merge with the Kingdom of Antichrist. They must submit to Lucifer as being the leading divinity. The authors actually put Jesus Christ in the place of Lucifer because they had Chang think in his mind that Jesus was the supreme potentate, or leading divinity. This is blasphemous.

No wonder God's wrath is on the Left Behind series. Jesus Christ is the ONLY potentate, not the leading divinity. Jesus

Christ is the King of Kings and Lord of Lords! He is not the supreme potentate or leading divinity. He is the ONLY potentate and the Most High who will live and reign in power and majesty forever and ever.

13

NEW AGE MARKINGS ON *LEFT BEHIND*

> The New Age Movement is a world wide group of organizations who have as their common goal a NEW AGE and a NEW CHRIST and a NEW DOCTRINE. They are bound together by mystical experiences.[1]

The *Left Behind* series has a new "Christ," new and unbiblical doctrines, and mystical, New Age experiences. This is not surprising because the official *Left Behind* website had for a long time on their site a "gospel presentation" called "The Plan," which contains New Age[2] elements. At this writing the archives are accessible on the internet.[3]

Having Premonitions Is Not Walking in the Spirit

A premonition is an anticipation of an event without a conscious reason. An unbeliever will have premonitions, or leadings from sources of which he is not aware but a walking-in-the-Spirit Christian will not. He will know the voice of his Lord because Jesus said, "My sheep hear my voice, and I know them, and they follow me" (John 10:27).

The authors left out the genuine Bible doctrine that a Christian must be led of the Holy Spirit and replaced it with a satanic counterfeit – a "premonition" – which they passed off as the true led-of-the-Spirit teaching.

Chloe warned Buck about her fearful premonition regarding his overnight accommodations:

> "Honey, I don't know how to tell you this, but I just have this feeling that you should not be in that hotel tonight. In fact, I just have a premonition that you shouldn't be in Jerusalem overnight. I don't know about tomorrow, and I don't know about premonitions and all that, but the feeling is so strong –" (*Nicolae*, pp. 185-86)

Right after the exchange about the premonition, the authors' narration went on to reveal Buck's thoughts about walking in the Spirit, thus deliberately associating premonitions with the bible doctrine "walk in the Spirit."

> Buck didn't know what he thought about this new level of what Bruce had referred to as "walking in the spirit." (*Nicolae*, p. 186)

Anyone can have a premonition, but only the saints of God can walk in the Spirit. Premonitions and walking in the Spirit are *not* the same thing, and this is one of many places in the series where the authors mix together what is of God and what is of Satan. Please notice that the authors used a small "s" in the phrase "walking in the spirit." "Walk in the Spirit," which appears twice in scripture, has a capital "S" for Holy Spirit. Putting a small "s" in the phrase "walk in the spirit" takes away the proper noun of Holy Spirit and makes the spirit any spirit – even a demon spirit – which could be the one giving the premonition.

Here is another example of the word premonition being used in *Nicolae*. Loretta explained to Chloe and Buck the circumstances surrounding Bruce's death, and the authors chose to use the New Age catchword "premonition" twice in this conversation as well:

> "Bruce told me they were taking him out of the emergency room and straight to intensive care, so he wouldn't be able to have any visitors for a while. I think he had a premonition."
> "A premonition?" Buck said.
> "I think he knew he might die," she said. (*Nicolae*, p. 29)

It was unnecessary to use the word "premonition" in this conversation. Loretta could have said that Bruce thought he might die; there was no need to put New Age markings on it.

During the Tribulation, the saints of the Most High *must* be led of the Holy Spirit, which is to *know* the voice of their Shepherd, the Lord Jesus Christ. "For as many as are led by the Spirit of God, they are the sons of God" (Rom 8:14). Anyone can have a premonition. *Only* the sons of God are led of the Spirit of God. Premonitions can be had by the children of darkness. Do not be deceived into thinking that having premonitions has the same meaning as walking in the Spirit. "Beloved, believe not every spirit, but try the spirits whether they are of God" (see 1 John 4:1).

Prayer Circles: Witchcraft

Praying in a circle with hands clasped is becoming common in churches and Christian homes today. This is not a biblical practice but has been adopted because of the infiltration into the churches by occultists who have pushed to get the church to accept this and other occult practices into worship services.

Tribulation Force depicts a situation in which a small group of Christians held hands in a circle and prayed:

> Before they parted, they held hands in a circle and prayed yet again. (*Tribulation Force*, p. 426)

Prayer circles are not found in scripture, and are used in witchcraft to make contact with spirits that are not of God.[4] Let us look at Bruce's prayer while he was in his "prayer circle" before I comment further:

> "Father," Bruce whispered, "for this brief flash of joy in a world on the brink of disaster, we thank you and pray your blessing and protection on us all until we meet back here again. Bind our hearts as brothers and sisters in Christ while we are apart." (*Tribulation Force*, p. 426)

Bruce did not pray to his Heavenly Father, but only to "Father." He also did not pray in Jesus' name. The authors did not even try to add any Christian flavor to this occultic-looking prayer circle. Satan would have been pleased by this prayer because it was done in a circle with the participants holding hands, there was no specific mention of the *Heavenly* Father, and the petitions were not made in Jesus' name.

Desecration Promotes Meditation

Transcendental meditation is central to the New Age movement. The authors depicted George, a Christian, using transcendental meditation (in the place of prayer) during his interrogation. He used this occultic technique so he could attempt to blot from his mind the reality of what was happening:

> "It hadn't worked long then, and that was what he feared now. This was the real thing. While he regulated his breathing and told himself not to think about his hunger and thirst, they were things he could not blot from his mind. (*Desecration*, p. 374)

The fact that the meditation techniques did not work does not excuse the fact that they presented a Christian practicing transcendental meditation. The authors even went so far as to try to deceive the reader into believing that meditation can be a non-religious activity:

> Even back then, before becoming a believer in Christ, he didn't want anything to do with any religious aspects of meditation. (*Desecration*, pp. 373-74)

Transcendental meditation is a religious activity no matter how it is disguised. The published writings of Maharishi say that:

> "Transcendental Meditation is a path to God."[5]

The "God" to which transcendental meditation leads is not the God of the Holy Bible, but Satan. The "God" of transcendental meditation poses as God and gives peaceful feelings in exchange for the soul of the one enticed into embracing him in this manner.

Calling Jesus "The One"

Jesus was called "The One" in Chaim's sermons:

> "He is the only One who could be Messiah," Chaim proclaimed. (*Desecration*, p. 231)

> "Of the billions and billions of people who have ever lived, One stands head and shoulders above the rest in terms of influence." (*Desecration*, p. 231)

Gail Riplinger exposed the meaning of "the One" in her revealing book, *New Age Bible Versions*:
1. 'The One' or 'the Only One' is Lucifer, the angel of this planet's evolution.
2. 'The One' or 'the Living One' is all of reality as described in pantheism or monism.
3. 'The Coming One' or 'The Mighty One' is Lord Maitreya's New Age Christ [antichrist].[6]

Calling Jesus "the One" may be the norm in the churches, but that is because they are falling away from the true Jesus. "The One" is the title for Lucifer, and Christians must not plunge into the falling away by substituting Lucifer's title for the name of the Lord Most High. There is definitely none like our God, but the New Agers want you to think there is One that is our God.

Jesus Designated a New Age Title: "Coming One"

Pastor Demetrius Demeter explained to Rayford that God had uniquely gifted and blessed him. He considered himself likely to be one of the 144,000 Jewish evangelists, and that makes his statements which I will quote all the more dangerous because of the "appeal to authority" propaganda technique used here. Pastor Demeter is someone the reader will pay close attention to and what he had to say is New Age to the core:

> "I have loved the Scriptures since long before I was aware that Jesus fit all the prophecies of the Coming One." (*The Indwelling*, p. 107)

> Today there is an increasing expectancy regarding the return of the "World Teacher;" the Coming One who will return to lead humanity into a new age and into a heightened consciousness.[7]

The Coming One is *not* the Holy Jesus of the Bible; he is the New Age "Christ." What is more, death will fulfill his purpose:

> In the "The Great Invocation", a "prayer" highly reverenced among New Agers and chanted to "invoke" the Maitreya, says, "Let Light and Love and Power and Death, Fulfill the purpose of the Coming One."[8]

Pastor Demeter made another New-Age-marked statement that particularly illustrates my statement in the introduction that the *Left Behind* series is finishing off the falling away of the church:

> I had been merely bemused by the idea that the Gentiles, specifically Christians, thought they had a corner on our theology. Then the Rapture occurred and I was not only forced to study Jesus in a different light, but I was also irresistibly drawn to him." (*The Indwelling,* p. 107)

This statement, made by an authority figure who previously designated Jesus as the New Age Christ ("The Coming One"), said that after the Rapture occurred he was forced to study Jesus in a different light. Ostensibly this could be because he was Jewish and never considered Jesus before. However, because he dubbed Jesus Christ with the same name New Agers call their "Christ" and by his statement that he was forced to study Jesus in a different light, the reader must beware.

Jesus must be studied only in the light of God's Word. To call Jesus "The Coming One" and then to say you were forced to study Jesus in a different light (after the disappearances) is a major reason this book is being written.

Jesus Christ is being presented in the *Left Behind* series, not in the light of the Word of God, but in a mixture of light and darkness. Because God has no darkness in Him at all, we know the "God" of the Left Behind series is not the God of the Holy Bible.

May none of us succumb to the delusion of studying Jesus in a "new light," which is exactly what the Illuminists hope we would do. They want us enlightened or illumined to accept another Jesus and another gospel which will initiate us into the New Age Kingdom of Antichrist.

Jesus is God; Jesus is Not God?

Satan knows that if he presents lies by themselves they will be recognized as such and rejected. That is why he presents truth and then sprinkles lies into the truth so that his lies will not be easily detected. The authors presented Jesus as being God on several occasions in the *Left Behind* series. However, they also implied the New Age belief that Jesus is not God:

> Here he was in the Holy Land thinking about God, thinking about Jesus, communicating with the two witnesses, trying to steer clear of the Antichrist and his cohorts. (*Nicolae*, p. 175)

> Dr. Ben-Judah explained God and Jesus and the Rapture and the Tribulation so clearly that I desperately wanted to believe. (*Assassins*, p. 37)

There are other examples but I have room in this chapter for only one more:

> "We have served the Lord God Almighty, maker of heaven and earth, and Jesus Christ, his only begotten son." (*Assassins*, p. 369)

Christians are sons of God; Jesus Christ is the only begotten *Son* of God. They used a small "s" on this occasion which denotes Jesus as being a mere human, and not God.

Tsion Ben-Judah's New Age Experience of "Light"

Tsion Ben-Judah had two out-of-body experiences in *The Indwelling*. Much could be written about the fact that he did not test the spirits he was talking with, but merely took them at their word that they were angels. Also, he spent much time trying to get information from these spirits, which is a New Age practice. New Agers try to get information from their guiding spirits.

The following excerpt exposes Tsion's "experience of light" that he received by astral projection for the occultic initiation into the New Age it really was:

> For one to be part of the world servers in the New Age, they must first have an initiation. This does not come necessarily from joining a specific group, but by ones own spiritual experience. The common denominator for those who are enlightened is the experience of light. It does not matter how one receives it. Whether it comes by meditation, or a spirit guide or from their Astral travelling, as long as they have experienced it.[9]

Here are the passages from Tsion's first out-of-body experience that include references to "light:"

> And as if a switch had been pulled, the darkness turned to the brightest light, obliterating the utter darkness of space. (*The Indwelling*, p. 235)

> This light, like a burst of burning magnesium so powerful as to chase even a shadow, came from above and behind him. (*The Indwelling*, p. 235)

> The light seemed to beckon him, to will him to turn. And so he did. (*The Indwelling*, p. 235)

The authors presented the idea that this occultic experience might be Tsion seeing the manifestation of God:

> If this was the Shekinah glory, would he not die in its presence? (*The Indwelling*, p. 235)

In reality it was the manifestation of Lucifer, the light bearer.

Angels With Demonic Characteristics

The writers gave Michael the archangel demonic qualities:

> It was as if the mere mention of Antichrist had stoked his bloodlust for battle. (*The Indwelling*, p. 243)

Demons lust to do *their own will*, which is to murder; God's holy angels execute God's will, which is righteous judgment.

Tsion asked him if he was Jesus the Christ. Look at what the authors had the audacity to write in the prefacing narration:

> A rumble, a chuckle, a terrestrial laugh? (*The Indwelling*, p. 242)

A holy angel of God would never laugh if a person mistook him for being Jesus! He would soberly correct him. A demon, however, would mock Jesus by laughing at the mention of His name.

Michael the archangel speaks God's Words, not his own. This demonic "angel" in *The Indwelling* took credit for his own words, which is what a demon would do:

> "So have I spoken." (*The Indwelling*, p. 242)

An Angel Healed Rayford

> Rayford wondered if he was dreaming. He leaned toward the man as the man leaned toward him. "So, who are you? Rayford said.
> "I am Michael," he said. "I am here to restore and heal you."
> (*Desecration*, p. 235)

In the Bible, God heals, angels do not. In the New Age movement, demons disguised as angels heal. Another word for "healing angels" is "spirit guides" or "demons." Notice the authors did not have Rayford test this spirit. The spirit said it was Michael, and Rayford simply believed it in violation of the Bible's teaching to test the spirits:

> Beloved, believe not every spirit, but try the spirits whether they are of God: because many false prophets are gone out into the world.
> (1 John 4:1)

When the characters of the *Left Behind* series had "angelic" encounters, not once did any of them test the spirits to see if they were of God. Merely requiring the spirits to confess that Jesus Christ is the Lord is not enough to test the spirits. Demons will admit Jesus Christ is the Lord. The way to test these angels (spirits) would be to see if they would confess that Jesus Christ was *their own* Lord and the Most High God.

Acceding to Intuitive Side Equals Salvation?

In blatantly New Age narrative, the authors explained why Rayford was not saved earlier:

> What had happened to the scientific, logical Rayford, the one who had been left behind primarily due to that inability to accede to his intuitive side? (*The Indwelling*, p. 50)

Rayford trusted Tsion's intuition:

> Tsion had become convinced that Chaim was God's man for this time, and Rayford had learned to trust the rabbi's intuition. (*The Mark*, p. 309)

Intuition is a word used often in the New Age movement. It has nothing to do with Bible Christianity, where sons of God are led of the Spirit of God, not by intuition.

The *Left Behind* series became darker as the series progressed. They did not make such blatantly New Age statements in the earlier novels in the series.

Jesus' Crucifixion: A Martyrdom?

The authors went so far as to depict Jesus' death on the cross to pay for the sins of the world as a martyrdom:

> Centuries after his public unmerciful mocking, his persecution and martyrdom, billions claimed membership in his church, making it by far the largest religion in the world. (*Desecration*, p. 231)

This is definitely an unscriptural view of Jesus Christ's death. Jesus never called himself a martyr. He said what no martyr could ever say:

> Jesus answered and said unto them, Destroy this temple, and in three days I will raise it up. (John 2:19)

He was referring, of course, to the temple of His body. No martyr can raise his own body from the grave, and no martyr's blood was shed for the remission of sins.

Paul never referred to Jesus as a martyr, and you will not find this taught anywhere in scripture. Viewing Jesus' death as a martyrdom will not save sinners:

> "Stephen died a martyr's death but Paul never preached forgiveness through the death of Stephen. Such a view of Christ's death may beget martyrs, but it can never save sinners" [10]

The word martyr is not used in connection with Jesus' death. Only Christianity of the "falling away" kind would not protest when the crucifixion of their Lord and Savior is called a martyrdom.

14

SATAN'S SOUL HARVEST

Satan is harvesting souls through the teachings in the *Left Behind* series. The false gospel that produces false Christians is Satan's most effective tool to reap his harvest both now and during the tribulation. The following is a list of some of the satanic salvation teachings promoted in the *Left Behind* series. The page numbers are only a representative sampling.

Satan's "Send You to Hell" Teachings

1. You can refuse to be saved now and not receive the strong delusion promised by God to those who enter the tribulation still not believing the truth, but having pleasure in unrighteousness (see 2 Thess. 2:1-12).

2. You can believe Antichrist is God and still be saved later (*Left Behind*, pp. 308, 386; see examples of Leah in *Assassins*, pp. 94-96; and Hannah in *Desecration*, pp. 217-23).

3. The purpose of the tribulation is so that God can get the attention of those who previously scorned his salvation (*Apollyon*, pp. 303, 282, 261, 240, 161; *Assassins*, p. 334; *Soul Harvest*, pp. 108-09).

4. If you do not "disappear" before the tribulation, Jesus forgot you, and you can be certain you are not a Christian (*Left Behind*, p. 355).

5. You can deny Christ before men and still be saved (*Assassins*, pp. 38-39; *The Mark* 223).

6. You can confess Antichrist as the risen lord and still be saved (*The Mark*, p.164).

7. No matter what you do, whether be it murdering, envyings, hatred, strife, suicide, lying, stealing, coveting, revilings, selfishness, extortion, and even denying Jesus Christ before men, you will still be in the book of life because at one point in time you made a "transaction" with God. (*The Mark*, p. 149)

8. The *only difference* between a Christian and an unbeliever during the tribulation is that a Christian has one more way to die (*Left Behind*, p. 419).

9. There are no human rules for a Christian during the tribulation. (*Assassins*, p. 116).

10. You can pretend to be a part of Satan's Kingdom of Antichrist and still be saved. God will lead you to work for Antichrist. (*Tribulation Force,* p. 310)

11. Antichrist has no ability to affect Christians' minds, even if they are giving place to the devil through sinful living. Christians can even have satanists lay hands on them and they will not be spiritually harmed (*The Indwelling,* pp. 208-09).

12. God will motivate you to *not* confess Jesus Christ in order to save your own life during the tribulation (*Tribulation Force,* pp. 130-31).

13. Your name can never be blotted out of the book of life no matter how much you serve sin to save your own life during the tribulation (*The Mark,* p. 149).

14. You will not have the ability to take the mark of the beast. God will render you *incapable* of committing this soul-damning sin. This teaching is satanic to the core (*The Mark*, p. 339).

15. If you take the mark of the beast, you can still turn against Antichrist (*Desecration,* p. 388).

16. If you appear to be loyal to Antichrist, even to the point of the mark, you are still saved (*Desecration,* p. 380).
17. You are not a true Christian unless you have a visible cross mark on your forehead at some point during the tribulation. You will not be able to see your own mark, but others who have this mark (and are ostensibly Christians) will be able to see it (*Soul Harvest,* pp. 172-73; *Apollyon.* p. 196; *Assassins,* p. 211; *Desecration,* p. 233).
18. A person can be a Christian and hate others if they are stupid (*Desecration,* p. 266).
19. A Christian may lie; and even say "I swear" while lying (*Desecration,* p. 268) (see James 5:12).
20. If a person enters the tribulation not saved, it is because he did not accede to his intuitive side rather than because he was in rebellion to God. (*The Indwelling,* p. 50)
21. You can come to Jesus Christ for fire insurance – to stay out of hell (*The Indwelling,* p. 229).
22. God sees you as a Christian *through* His sinless Son. That is why Christians can serve unrighteousness (even commit murder) and still go to heaven (*The Mark,* p. 308). The truth is God *does* see the sins of Christians and certain sins cause them to not inherit the kingdom of God (see 1 Cor. 6:9-10; Gal. 5:19-21).
23. Since salvation is a gift from God, you can receive it and keep it on your own terms; not God's terms as clearly laid down in the Holy Bible. (See examples of this in many scenarios depicted in the *Left Behind* series.)

24. A Christian may pretend to pray to Antichrist and still be a follower of Jesus Christ (*The Indwelling,* p. 353).
25. If a person is saved first, nothing can separate him from the love of God – even if he does not confess Christ and receives the mark of the beast (*The Mark,* p. 354).
26. If a person has decided for Christ he cannot change his mind. (*The Mark,* p. 339) The Bible says we can draw back unto perdition (see Heb. 10:38-39).
27. God might put you on assignment to sin in order to serve Him, and if he does, he will automatically cleanse you from your sins while you are disobeying His Word and *not* "walking in the light" (*Assassins,* p. 68) (see 1 John 1:7).
28. You can take the Luciferic Initiation if you remind yourself to think about Jesus Christ while you are confessing with your mouth Antichrist. (*Desecration,* p. 322)

God-Sent Delusion; Not a God-Sent Revival

The tribulation will be just like the time of Noah. Just as people were doing their own will and refused to repent up to the day Noah entered the ark, it will be the same way when the tribulation begins. When God shut the door, it was too late for those outside of the ark.

This is exactly how God has said things will happen during the tribulation. Those who refuse to love the truth (whether "Christians" or unbelievers) but continue to enjoy their unrighteous lives will not repent when that Wicked is revealed, who is known in the Bible as that man of sin or the son of perdition. He is known in *Left Behind* series as the Antichrist.

What *Left Behind* proclaims is God's "attention-getter" is the exact opposite of what the Bible actually teaches. God will not only *not* get the attention of people who have already rejected the truth, he will judge them so they will be deceived into believing the lie: that Antichrist is God. People who insist on serving unrighteousness now and are therefore serving Satan will continue to serve him in the tribulation – God will see to it. God will not be mocked and whatever a man sows before the tribulation, he will reap during it as well.

The *Left Behind* series gives the reader a false hope right out of the pit of hell, that you can serve sin today and then decide to serve Jesus when that Wicked is revealed. Now is the day of salvation. Just as there is no purgatory, or second chance after death to be saved, there is no second chance for loving the truth for those who entered the tribulation still scorning the salvation of Jesus Christ and having pleasure in unrighteousness. A second chance to get right with God after that Wicked reveals himself in the tribulation does not exist in the Holy Bible (see 2 Thess. 2:1-12).

People who believe the lie, that Antichrist is the real God, will not be able to be saved later. The reason for this is because "God shall send them strong delusion that they should believe a lie: that they all might be damned who believed not the truth, but had pleasure in unrighteousness" (2 Thess. 2:11-12). The *Left Behind* series teaches salvation when the Bible teaches it will be too late to receive it. Many souls will be destroyed by this false teaching unless great effort is made on the part of all real Christians to take back what has been given to Satan through the church's embracing of the *Left Behind* series. Hell is the most horrifying and sobering reality that exists. The teachings of the *Left Behind* series are causing the church to completely fall away from the faith of Jesus and draw back unto perdition which is hell:

> But we are not of them who draw back unto perdition; but of them that believe to the saving of the soul. (Heb. 10:39)

The falling away of the church is just what Satan connives to bring forth because he cannot bring in the tribulation until this event has taken place. The unbeliever, who probably picked these books up to learn of the things of God, is being presented with Satan disguised as God. The real God is holy and his real followers are holy just like Him:

> For God hath not called us unto uncleanness, but unto holiness. (1 Thess. 4:7)

> Follow peace with all men, and holiness, without which no man shall see the Lord (Heb. 12:14)

Please buy a King James Bible and read the New Testament. Every time you come to a verse that explains the behavior of the person who has been bought with the blood of Jesus, underline or highlight it. Read all the books slowly. Take note of everything God says in the Bible regarding salvation and keeping your salvation. Take note of the times Paul preached to the churches and told them that if they do these things they will not inherit the kingdom of God. The free gift of God which is eternal life through Jesus Christ our Lord cannot be earned or deserved. But the Bible also says that certain *works* can cause the Christian to not inherit the kingdom of God. The gift of God cannot be received and kept in contempt of the Giver's terms. God's people *can* fall away or depart from the true faith of Jesus (Heb. 6:6, 2 Pet. 3:17, Luke 8:13, 2 Thess. 2:3, 1 Tim.4:1, 1 Tim.1:19). God's people can also be cut off (Rom. 11:22). We *must* hold fast the faith of Jesus Christ steadfast until the end:

> For we are made partakers of Christ, if we hold the beginning of our confidence steadfast unto the end; (Heb.3:14)

Repenting of Fellowshipping With *Left Behind*

GOD'S WRATH on *Left Behind* has been written at the Lord's command to reprove or expose the works of darkness in the *Left Behind* series:

> And have no fellowship with the unfruitful works of darkness, but rather reprove them. (Eph. 5:11)

If you have had fellowship with the works of darkness by reading the *Left Behind* series you need to cast off this work of darkness and put on the armour of light:

> The night is far spent, the day is at hand: let us therefore cast off the works of darkness, and let us put on the armour of light. (Rom. 13:12)

The following is a suggested way to pray to the Lord to repent of having fellowship with devils through willingly taking in the doctrines of devils woven throughout the pages of the *Left Behind* series. You can use your own words, or you may use these words to help you:

Dear Heavenly Father,

I have engaged in reading books that have teachings that exalt themselves against the knowledge of your pure and Holy Word. You exalt your Word even above your name, and I have made light of your Word by enjoying fiction that blasphemes your Word by perverting it.

I have turned my ears away from the truth as written in your Word and have given heed to seducing spirits by believing fables which have caused me to question your Holy Word which endures forever. I have disobeyed your Word by not refusing the profane fables of the *Left Behind* series. I am sorry that I took sound doctrine lightly and have heaped to myself volumes of *Left Behind* books that are making merchandise of my soul and the souls of others I have directed to read these books.

I repent of disobeying your Word and not abstaining from the appearance of evil when it first showed itself in the *Left Behind* series. I did not care that your Word was being trifled with because I was enjoying myself and cared more about my pleasure than proving what is acceptable to You. I repent and turn from this sin and will do what I can to help others who have been spiritually harmed by the doctrines of devils taught in the *Left Behind* series.

Thank you for helping me see my sin, and thank you for forgiving me. Help me to continue in your word and be your disciple indeed. In Jesus precious name,

Amen.

Renouncing the Devilish Doctrines of *Left Behind*

> But have renounced the hidden things of dishonesty, not walking in craftiness, nor handling the word of God deceitfully; but by manifestation of the truth commending ourselves to every man's conscience in the sight of God. (2 Cor. 4:2)

You may use your own words or use these words to help you verbally renounce the hidden things of dishonesty cleverly woven into the text of the *Left Behind* series:

In the name of Jesus Christ I renounce all the examples and doctrines in the *Left Behind* series that exalt themselves against the knowledge of God and His Holy Word, the Bible. I specifically renounce the satanic teachings listed in this chapter. Every evil spirit that I have invited into my life by my sin of enjoying doctrines of devils must leave me in the name of Jesus Christ.

You need to take the time to go over the false teachings listed above and renounce them one at a time consciously and deliberately. The Holy Spirit might bring some to your mind that I have not mentioned in this chapter, and you must be sensitive to Him and renounce what He is impressing on your heart.

Bring Not This Doctrine into Your House

> Look to yourselves, that we lose not those things which we have wrought, but that we receive a full reward. Whosoever transgresseth, and abideth not in the doctrine of Christ, hath not God. He that abideth in the doctrine of Christ, he hath both the Father and the Son. If there come any unto you, and bring not this doctrine, receive him not into your house, neither bid him God speed: (2 John 1:8-10)

The *Left Behind* series does not abide in the doctrine of Christ and does not present the true Christ of the Bible. Will you keep these antichrist doctrines in your home and say, "God bless you" to them? May you obey the Holy Spirit as he leads you to apply this Bible passage according to the will of Jesus Christ.

THE GOSPEL: HOW TO BE SAVED

Man was created in the image of God

So God created man in his own image, in the image of God created he him; male and female created he them. (Genesis 1:27)

God created us so that we could walk with Him and worship Him. We were created to have fellowship with Almighty God.

All are sinners.
For all have sinned and come short of the glory of God. (Rom. 3:23)

Jesus Christ is God's one and only answer to sin.
Although we have all broken God's law and deserve death in hell, God has made a way for us in Jesus Christ.

For when we were yet without strength [dead in sin], in due time Christ died for the ungodly.
But God commendeth His love towards us, in that, while we were sinners, Christ died for us. (Rom. 5:6-8)

Christ died and shed His blood for our sins, and He rose again from the dead, taking authority over the power of sin and death Himself.

Jesus Christ is the *only* way to know God!
And Jesus saith unto him "I am the Way, the Truth, and the Life: no man cometh unto the Father but by me!" (John 14:6)

Jesus Christ is "God manifest in the flesh:"
"If ye had known me, ye should have known my Father also: and from henceforth ye know him, and have seen him...He that hath seen me hath seen the Father." (John 14:7-8)

Christ shed His blood and bore our sins on the cross at Calvary that we might be forgiven and cleansed and delivered from sin.

Christ was perfect in every way, yet to save our souls He offered himself to God the Father for our sins.

> In whom we have redemption through his blood, even the forgiveness of sins. (Col. 1:14)

> He [God the Father] hath made him [Jesus Christ his Son] to be sin for us, who knew no sin, that we might be the righteousness of God in him. (2 Cor. 5:21)

When we receive Christ into our lives we are born again and we are forgiven of our sins.

> If any man be in Christ, he is a new creature: old things are passed away; behold, all things are become new. (2 Cor. 5:17)

We are free to have a relationship with God and to live in His abundant life. Jesus said:

> "I am come that they might have life, and that they might have it more abundantly." (John 10:10)

If we reject Christ and his authority over our lives then we are still in our sins and doomed to an eternity in hell.

> He that believeth on Him [Christ] in not condemned: but he that believeth not is condemned already [because we are already in sin], because he hath not believed in the name of the Only-Begotten Son of God. (John 3:18)

But if we put our faith and trust in Christ we are saved from hell and we can know God right now. We can live in His abundant life and grace, and we can be filled with the Holy Ghost.

We are saved by faith in the life, death, and resurrection of the Lord Jesus Christ.
When we believe in Christ we become children of God.

> For as many as received him, to them gave he power to become sons of God, even to them that believe on his name. (John 1:12)

We must receive Christ by faith. When we have faith in what the Bible says about Jesus, and that He died for our sins, we are forgiven, and justified before God. We cannot be saved by good works. We must have faith in Jesus Christ's blood atonement for our sins, and that His righteousness alone can save us.

> For by grace are ye saved, through faith; and not of your-selves: it is a gift of God: Not of works, lest any man should boast. For we are his workmanship, created in Christ Jesus unto good works, which God hath before ordained that we should walk in them. (Eph. 2:8-10)

> Much more then, being now justified by his blood, we shall be saved from wrath through him. (Rom.5:9)

In order to be born again we must repent (turn completely from sin), and believe in Christ. This is the gospel message.

In order to receive salvation we must believe in Christ and confess Him as our own Lord and Savior.

> If thou shalt confess with thy mouth the Lord Jesus. And believe in thine heart that God hath raised him from the dead, thou shalt be saved. For with the heart man believeth unto righteousness; and with the mouth confession is made unto salvation. (Rom. 10:9-10)

Salvation is available to anyone who is willing to accept Christ as their LORD and SAVIOR, and to be obedient to Him.

In you want to receive the love of God and the forgiveness of your sins by accepting the Lord Jesus Christ by faith you must call on Jesus in sincere faith and repentance.

Now, take time to repent of your sins. Confess them one by one to Christ so that he can cleanse you and deliver you from every sin. Continue to pray until you know that your sins have been forgiven and that Jesus Christ is your Lord and Savior. Let the Spirit of God bear witness to your spirit that you are a child of God.

In order to know God you must read the Bible. It is God's infallible Word.

> But the word of the Lord endureth forever. And this is the word which by the gospel is preached unto you. (1 Pet. 1:25)

The Bible is the power of God to save your soul and give you power over sin. The Bible is God made known to man.

> I am not ashamed of the Gospel of Jesus Christ: for it is the power of God unto salvation to every one that believeth. (Rom. 1:16)

Without the Bible we cannot know God and we will fall out of fellowship with him.

> My people are destroyed for lack of knowledge [knowledge of God and his word]. (Hosea 4:6)

We must also learn to pray to God. Prayer is talking to God and exercising your relationship with him. In prayer we should worship and exalt God and pray for others. We must pray continually and perpetually lift up the name of Jesus.

Finally we must join a Holy Ghost-filled, Bible-Believing Church. When we are saved the Bible says we are joined to the body of Christ, his church. In order to grow in our faith and to learn about Jesus Christ, we must join with other believers. We must love one another and encourage one another.

> But exhort one another daily, while it called Today; lest any one of you be hardened through the deceitfulness of sin. (Heb. 3:13-14)

For we are made partakers of Christ, if we hold the beginning of our confidence steadfast *unto the end.*

Andy Wehrheim
The Apostolic Bible Church of the Lord Jesus Christ
http://members.boardhost.com/JesusReigns/

> Author's note: Because we are living in the time of the falling away of the church from the true faith of Jesus, it is very important to seek God's specific leading before joining in spiritual fellowship with a congregation of believers.

WHAT DOES IT MEAN TO BE A TRUE CHRISTIAN?

First of all we must establish the spiritual reality that there are two and only two spiritual kingdoms, no more and absolutely no less. They are the Kingdom of God, also called the Kingdom of Heaven and the Kingdom of Darkness, Satan's kingdom. In John 8:44 Jesus told religious leaders of His day that rejected Him, "Ye are of your father the devil." Everyone has a spiritual father; depending on which kingdom he is a part of.

The second spiritual fact is that we are born in sin and therefore not born into the Kingdom of God. Psalm 51:5 "Behold, I was shapen in iniquity; and in sin did my mother conceive me." To enter into the Kingdom of God we have to be 'born again.' John 3:3 "Jesus answered and said unto him, Verily, verily, I say unto thee, Except a man be born again, he cannot see the kingdom of God." John 3:5-6 "Jesus answered, Verily, verily, I say unto thee, Except a man be born of water and of the Spirit, he cannot enter into the kingdom of God. That which is born of the flesh is flesh; and that which is born of the Spirit is spirit."

When we come to Christ and receive His salvation, we are transferred from one kingdom to another. Colossians 1:13 "Who hath delivered us from the power of darkness, and hath translated us into the kingdom of his dear Son."

The third spiritual fact is that each kingdom has a king and that king rules over his kingdom, those who are his subjects. Have you ever heard of an earthly kingdom in which the king did not have power and authority over his subjects? That authority and power is what makes him a king. And the king has servants to enforce his rule over his subjects. Matthew 6:24 "No man can serve two masters: for either he will hate the one, and love the other; or else he will hold to the one, and despise the other. Ye cannot serve God and mammon." Matthew 12:25 "And Jesus knew their thoughts, and said unto them, Every kingdom divided against itself is brought to desolation; and every city or house divided against itself shall not stand."

Some men would say that they don't believe in God or the Devil and they don't serve either. The spiritual fact and reality is that they are deceived, for you don't have a choice and are by birth and nature a child of the devil. To refuse to serve God is to be under the kingdom of darkness. 2 Corinthians 4:4 "In whom the god of this world hath blinded the minds of them which believe not, lest the light of the glorious gospel of Christ, who is the image of God, should shine unto them." So we see that Satan is the god of this world. Those who have come to Christ are no longer citizens and a part of this world. John 8:23 "And he said unto them, Ye are from beneath; I am from above: ye are of this world; I am not of this world." John 18:36 "Jesus answered, My kingdom is not of this world: if my kingdom were of this world, then would my servants fight, that I should not be delivered to the Jews: but now is my kingdom not from hence."

You are either of the earthly kingdom or of the heavenly kingdom. John 17:9 "I pray for them: I pray not for the world, but for them which thou hast given me; for they are thine." John 17:14 "I have given them thy word; and the world hath hated them, because they are not of the world, even as I am not of the world."

Now that we have established the spiritual fact that there are only two kingdoms and that each has a king and his subjects are subject to the authority and power of the king whom they are under, even more so that the subjects of a physical monarch or king have been subject to their king in this world, we must now consider the fact of what it is to be a part of the Kingdom of God and why those who reject Christ end up in eternal damnation.

In the spiritual realm, it is all about lordship. Who is lord over your life? Who sits on the throne of your life and has ultimate control of your life? If your answer to those questions is "I am", then you are a spiritual rebel and not under the authority or Lordship of Christ and therefore not a part of His Kingdom. John 13:16 "Verily, verily, I say unto you, The servant is not greater than his lord; neither he that is sent greater than he that sent him." Jesus is Lord in His Kingdom and we are His servants, which means we surrender control and final say of our lives to Him to become His workmanship. Ephesians 2:10 "For we are his workmanship, created in Christ Jesus unto good works, which God hath before ordained that we should walk in them." Philippians 2:13 "For it is God which worketh in you both to will and to do of his good pleasure." If that is not true and your are not His workmanship, but you are making your own decisions and telling God what you want to do and what you want Him to do for you, then you have it all reversed and are trying to be lord and make Him as your servant.

The subject and servant bows before His master and submits to His will. As in the natural, so it is in the spiritual. Luke 9:23 "And he said to them all, If any man will come after me, let him deny himself, and take up his cross daily, and follow me." Luke 14:27 "And whosoever doth not bear his cross, and come after me, cannot be my disciple." What does this mean? What is it to 'take up your cross'? First of all you are required to 'deny self'. That tells you that you have to deny your own self-will and therein is your cross. As Jesus in the Garden of Gethsemane, when He had to deny His own will as a human, as a man, to do the will of the Father, which was to go to the cross. Luke 22:42 "Saying, Father, if thou be willing, remove this cup from me: nevertheless not my will, but thine, be done." You cannot take up the will of God for your life and do it, until you have first laid down your own will. Your cross is not a person, a sickness, but the Will of God for your life that you don't want to do any more than the man Jesus wanted to go to the cross and die that horrible death. John 12:26 "If any man serve me, let him follow me; and where I am, there shall also my servant be: if any man serve me, him will my Father honour." Is it becoming clear yet?

How about this scripture: John 13:14a "If I then, your Lord and Master…" Jesus claimed to be Lord and Master to His disciples. Most today want to claim Jesus as Savior, but not as Lord over their lives. I have been told, "Well, I've made Jesus my Savior, but

I haven't made Him Lord of my life yet." Wrong! If He is not Lord, He is not savior! Scripture always puts His Lordship before His being Savior. 2 Peter 1:11 "For so an entrance shall be ministered unto you abundantly into the everlasting kingdom of our *Lord and Saviour* Jesus Christ." 2 Peter 2:20 "For if after they have escaped the pollutions of the world through the knowledge of the *Lord and Saviour* Jesus Christ, they are again entangled therein, and overcome, the latter end is worse with them than the beginning." 2 Peter 3:2 "That ye may be mindful of the words which were spoken before by the holy prophets, and of the commandment of us the apostles of the *Lord and Saviour:*" 2 Peter 3:18 "But grow in grace, and in the knowledge of our *Lord and Saviour* Jesus Christ. To him be glory both now and for ever. Amen." As a man of God once said and is often repeated, "If He is not Lord of ALL, then He is not Lord at all."

Look at what the Apostles themselves said of their own relationship to Jesus. Romans 1:1 "Paul, a servant of Jesus Christ, called to be an apostle, separated unto the gospel of God." Titus 1:1 "Paul, a servant of God, and an apostle of Jesus Christ, according to the faith of God's elect, and the acknowledging of the truth which is after godliness." James 1:1 "James, a servant of God and of the Lord Jesus Christ, to the twelve tribes which are scattered abroad, greeting." 2 Peter 1:1 "Simon Peter, a servant and an apostle of Jesus Christ, to them that have obtained like precious faith with us through the righteousness of God and our Saviour Jesus Christ." Jude 1:1 "Jude, the servant of Jesus Christ, and brother of James, to them that are sanctified by God the Father, and preserved in Jesus Christ, and called." In every case the Greek word for servant is doulos (doo'-los) and this is Strong's defines it as: "a *slave* (literal or figurative, involuntary or voluntary; frequently therefore in a qualified sense of *subjection* or *subserviency*):- bond (-man), servant."

1 Corinthians 2:8 "Which none of the princes of this world knew: for had they known it, they would not have crucified the *Lord of glory*." James 2:1 "My brethren, have not the faith of our *Lord Jesus Christ*, the *Lord of glory*, with respect of persons."

Revelation 19:16 "And he hath on his vesture and on his thigh a name written, *KING OF KINGS, AND LORD OF LORDS.*" Ultimately it will end up this way; "But those mine enemies, which would not that I should reign over them, bring hither, and slay them before me (Luke 19:27). All those in heaven bow before the Lord and worship and serve Him. That is what heaven is all about. Revelation 4:10-11 "The four and twenty elders fall down before him that sat on the throne, and worship him that liveth for ever and ever, and cast their crowns before the throne, saying. Thou art worthy, O Lord, to receive glory and honour and power: for thou hast created all things, and for thy pleasure they are and were created." Revelation 5:11-12 "And I beheld, and I heard the voice of many angels round about the throne and the beasts and the elders: and the number of them was ten thousand times ten thousand, and thousands of thousands; Saying with a loud voice, Worthy is the Lamb that was slain to receive power, and riches, and wisdom, and strength, and honour, and glory, and blessing."

We were created by Him and for Him. Colossians 1:16 "For by him were all things created, that are in heaven, and that are in earth, visible and invisible, whether they be thrones, or dominions, or principalities, or powers: all things were created by him, and for him." We exist for His pleasure and that we might have fellowship with Him and worship Him. Those on earth who are not submitted to His Lordship, who do not serve and worship Him here, would not at all be at 'home' in heaven or comfortable there. In eternity men will not love what they hate here or hate what they love here. Whatever we love and are here, we will be in eternity, only magnified. Revelation 22:11 "He that is unjust, let him be unjust still: and he which is filthy, let him be filthy still: and he that is righteous, let him be righteous still: and he that is holy, let him be holy still." So don't think that you can live unholy lives here and then you will be holy, that you can live for yourself here and you will want to live for God in eternity. It just isn't that way. It's those who love and want to please and serve Him, will be able to do so without hindrance, without temptation, without having the fallen nature of sin because of this flesh and those who are evil will be fully given over to the sin they love without anything to restrict or hinder them and their lusts will consume them in hell. Those who live in sin will not be able to stand His presence or to look at His face. They will say; "And said to the mountains and rocks, Fall on us, and hide us from the face of him that sitteth on the throne, and from the wrath of the Lamb (Revelation 6:16)."

This spiritual reality is why we were told such things as: 1 John 2:15-17 "Love not the world, neither the things that are in the world. If any man love the world, the love of the Father is *not* in him. For all that is in the world, the lust of the flesh, and the lust of the eyes, and the pride of life, is *not* of the Father, but is of the world. And the world passeth away, and the lust thereof: but he that doeth the will of God abideth for ever. " Remember, to do the will of God that is in contrast or contradiction to your own will, you have to be able to take up His will and you can't do that until you have laid down your own.

This is but the beginning of what it is to be a True Christian. This is where it begins, when a person surrenders their life to the Lord Jesus Christ and invites Him into their heart and life as Lord and Savior, not just as Savior. Romans 10:9-10 "That if thou shalt confess with thy mouth *the Lord Jesus*, and shalt believe in thine heart that God hath raised him from the dead, thou shalt be saved. For with the heart man believeth unto righteousness; and with the mouth confession is made unto salvation." This confession is not what most professors of religion think. It is not to confess that Jesus is Lord, not a metal ascent to a fact, but a personal confession of Him as your personal Lord, as Lord to you! As the Song goes; "Jesus, Jesus, Lord to me. Master, Savior, Prince of Peace. Ruler of my heart today. Jesus, Lord to me." That's what it means. You are confessing that He is not only Lord, but you put your faith in Him and trust Him as your Lord, as you surrender your life to Him. You cannot leave out the fact that coming to Christ and confessing Him as Lord and Savior also includes Repentance! That was the first thing Jesus preached. Matthew 4:17 "From that time Jesus began to preach, and to say, Repent: for the kingdom of heaven is at hand." Mark 1:15 "And saying, The time is fulfilled, and the kingdom of God is at hand: repent ye, and believe the gospel." Matthew 9:13 "But go ye and learn what that meaneth, I will have mercy, and not sacrifice: for I am not come to call the righteous, but sinners to repentance." *The beginning of repentance is that we are repenting of living our lives independently from God without considering Him in our daily choices of life.* That is our big sin, rejecting His Lordship. To reject His Lordship is to reject Him. To reject Him as Lord is to reject Him as Savior. You can't have it both ways. You can't have the benefits and blessing of being a part of His Kingdom without coming under the authority of the King.

Most think that Jesus just died for their sins, but not so, it only begins there. 2 Corinthians 5:15 "And that he died for all, that they which live should *not* henceforth live unto themselves, but unto him which died for them, and rose again." 1 Peter 4:2-4 "That he no longer should live the rest of his time in the flesh to the lusts of men, but to the will of God. For the time past of our life may suffice us to have wrought the will of the Gentiles, when we walked in lasciviousness, lusts, excess of wine, revellings, banquetings, and abominable idolatries: Wherein they think it strange that ye run not with them to the same excess of riot, speaking evil of you."

We are not to be as natural men who are unsaved and know not the Lord Jesus Christ when we have come to Him. Ephesians 2:1-3 "And you hath he quickened, who were dead in trespasses and sins; Wherein in time past ye walked according to the course of this world, according to the prince of the power of the air, the spirit that now worketh in the children of disobedience: Among whom also we all had our conversation in times past in the lusts of our flesh, fulfilling the desires of the flesh and of the mind; and were by nature the children of wrath, even as others."

Ephesians 4:17-32 "This I say therefore, and testify in the Lord, that ye henceforth walk not as other Gentiles walk, in the vanity of their mind, Having the understanding darkened, being alienated from the life of God through the ignorance that is in them, because of the blindness of their heart: Who being past feeling have given themselves over unto lasciviousness, to work all uncleanness with greediness. But ye have not so learned Christ; If so be that ye have heard him, and have been taught by him, as the truth is in Jesus: That ye put off concerning the former conversation the old man, which is corrupt according to the deceitful lusts; And be renewed in the spirit of your mind; And that ye put on the new man, which after God is created in righteousness and true holiness. Wherefore putting away lying, speak every man truth with his neighbour: for we are members one of another. Be ye angry, and sin not: let not the sun go down upon your wrath: Neither give place to the devil. Let him that stole steal no more: but rather let him labour, working with his hands the thing which is good, that he may have to give to him that needeth. Let no corrupt communication proceed out of your mouth, but that which is good to the use of edifying, that it may minister grace unto the hearers. And grieve not the holy Spirit of God, whereby ye are sealed unto the day of redemption. Let all bitterness, and wrath, and anger, and clamour, and evil speaking, be put away from you, with all malice: And be ye kind one to another, tenderhearted, forgiving one another, even as God for Christ's sake hath forgiven you."

There are hundreds of such verses and admonitions in scripture about and for the believer that tells us how we are to live and walk and what true Christianity is before God. If we Love the Lord Jesus, we will love our brothers and walk in His love. We will also walk in forgiveness and in mercy. We will not hate or hold grudges and unforgiveness. Those who do those things do not inherit the kingdom of God as many others.

That is the last thing I want to touch on. So many think that because they have 'confessed Jesus' or made a 'confession or profession of faith' that they can still keep living sinful lives and get by with it saying, 'God doesn't see my sin, He just sees the blood. No, He sees that you are a goat and not of His sheep. You aren't walking in grace, but Grease.

Titus 2:11-14 "For the grace of God that bringeth salvation hath appeared to all men, Teaching us that, denying ungodliness and worldly lusts, we should live soberly, righteously, and godly, in this present world; Looking for that blessed hope, and the glorious appearing of the great God and our Saviour Jesus Christ; Who gave himself for us, that he might redeem us from all iniquity, and purify unto himself a peculiar people, zealous of good works." The profession of faith is for those who are already 'born again' and belong to Christ and not the means of or way to salvation. 1 Timothy 6:12 "Fight the good fight of faith, lay hold on eternal life, whereunto thou art also called, and hast professed a good profession before many witnesses." And notice the necessity of continuance in fighting the fight of faith to lay hold of, not something that is automatic, guaranteed, with no cost or effort or work on your part. You enter into and receive salvation as a free gift, but it will cost you something to walk in it and keep it.

God has given us lists of those whom He says do not inherit or enter into the Kingdom of God and are not His own. John 10:14 "I am the good shepherd, and know my sheep, and am known of mine." John 10:27 "My sheep hear my voice, and I know them, and they follow me." Those who do not hear His voice and follow Him are goats and not sheep. Spiritual Goats do not inherit the kingdom.

1 Corinthians 6:9-11 "Know ye not that the unrighteous shall not inherit the kingdom of God? Be not deceived: neither fornicators, nor idolaters, nor adulterers, nor effeminate, nor abusers of themselves with mankind, Nor thieves, nor covetous, nor drunkards, nor revilers, nor extortioners, shall inherit the kingdom of God. And such were some of you: but ye are washed, but ye are sanctified, but ye are justified in the name of the Lord Jesus, and by the Spirit of our God." Galatians 5:13-25 "For, brethren, ye have been called unto liberty; only use not liberty for an occasion to the flesh, but by love serve one another. For all the law is fulfilled in one word, even in this; Thou shalt love thy neighbour as thyself. But if ye bite and devour one another, take heed that ye be not consumed one of another. This I say then,

Walk in the Spirit, and ye shall not fulfil the lust of the flesh. For the flesh lusteth against the Spirit, and the Spirit against the flesh: and these are contrary the one to the other: so that ye cannot do the things that ye would. But if ye be led of the Spirit, ye are not under the law. Now the works of the flesh are manifest, which are these; Adultery, fornication, uncleanness, lasciviousness, Idolatry, witchcraft, hatred, variance, emulations, wrath, strife, seditions, heresies, Envyings, murders, drunkenness, revellings, and such like: of the which I tell you before, as I have also told you in time past, that they which do such things shall not inherit the kingdom of God. But the fruit of the Spirit is love, joy, peace, longsuffering, gentleness, goodness, faith, Meekness, temperance: against such there is no law. And they that are Christ's have crucified the flesh with the affections and lusts. If we live in the Spirit, let us also walk in the Spirit."

I pray that you have given your heart and life to the giver of life and found eternal life in Him and begun to walk in that life. We don't enter eternal life in heaven, we enter and begin walking in it here and now, when we surrender to the Lordship of Jesus Christ.

Art Renz

The Shepherd's Voice
http://www.geocities.com/Heartland/Acres/3422/

Notes

Referenced footnotes are for documentation purposes only. The author does not necessarily endorse all the contents of any particular website listed except for her own site at www.libertytothecaptives.net

CHAPTER 1 – THE ANTI-CHRISTIAN GOSPEL OF *LEFT BEHIND*

[1] *Webster's 1828 Dictionary*
[2] Art Renz, Sermon: "What it Means to Be a True Christian"
 See also: http://www.geocities.com/Heartland/Acres/3422/
[3] Ralph Bouma, *Why Confusion Reigns* (Triangle Press, Conrad, MT, 1996) p. 43
[4] Diane Dew, *Essentials of the Christian Faith*
 (Diane Dew, Milwaukee, WI, 1982) p. 33
 http://www.dianedew.com
[5] Ibid.
[6] William C. Nichols, *The Gospel and Martyrdom,* (Chapel Library, A Ministry of Mt. Zion Bible Church, Pensacola, FL), p. 2
[7] Ibid, p. 4

CHAPTER 2 – ENTERTAINMENT: THE BEST TOOL FOR PROPAGANDA

[1] Steven M. Debock, Media Pollution Survival Course
 http://www.medialiteracy.net/research/pdfs/survivalcourse.pdf
[2] Propaganda Techniques
 http://www.freerepublic.com/forum/a360d496e0c97.htm
[3] Ibid.
[4] Ibid.
[5] Ibid.
[6] Ibid.
7 Jacques Ellul, Propaganda: The Formation of Men's Attitudes, (Vintage Books, New York, 1965) p. 35

CHAPTER 4 – *NICOLAE* AND PRO-ABORTION PROPAGANDA

[1] AfterAbortion.org
 http://nichole.simonweb.com/~afterabortion/awsnm.html

CHAPTER 6 –DISAPPEARANCES: THE BEST-KEPT SECRET

[1] *Left Behind*, pp. 16, 17, 22, 26, 28, 29, 30, 34, 35, 44, 45, 53, 96, 102, 110, 118, 119, 126, 148, 150, 159, 164 176, 194, 203, 207 209, 214, 242, 245, 253, 266, 281, 299, 304, 313, 325, 343, 344, 351, 356, 357, 363, 364, 370, 372, 379, 395, 411, 415, 422, 431, 433, 440
[2] The Science of Modern Propaganda
http://propaganda101.com/newpage81.htm
[3] The Science of Modern Propaganda
http://propaganda101.com/newpage111.htm
[4] Human Rights Watch
http://www.hrw.org/press98/june/indo0622.htm
[5] Ibid.
[6] The Lesser Unpleasantries of the Twentieth Century
http://users.erols.com/mwhite28/warstat5.htm
[7] Freedom's Nest
http://www.freedomsnest.com/rummel_totals.html
[8] The Plan in Action
http://notendur.centrum.is/~snorrigb/plan1.htm
[9] Let Us Reason Ministries
The Plan
http://www.letusreason.org/NAM20.htm
[10] Out of Body Experiences
http://www.drbrucegoldberg.com/newlart3.htm
[11] The Cutting Edge
http://www.cuttingedge.org/ce1013.html
[12] Ibid.
[13] Bible Believers.org,
November 1991
http://www.biblebelievers.org.au/nv2.htm
[14] TSG Foundation
http://www.tsg-publishing.com/booklets/hierarchy.htm
[15] New World Order Quotes
Ted Turner CNN Interview with Larry King 1997
http://www.amerikanexpose.com/quotes1.html
[16] The Cutting Edge
http://www.cuttingedge.org/news/n1378.cfm
[17] Left Behind.com
http://www.leftbehind.com/community/talk/sub.asp?item_id=712)
[18] Good News Ministry
Revealing the New Age
http://www3.bc.sympatico.ca/thegoodnews/newage.htm

Chapter 7 - The Bible On The Mark Of The Beast

[1] Diane Dew, *Essential Doctrines of the Christian Faith*
http://www.dianedew.com, p. 104

Chapter 9 – Satan On The Mark Of The Beast

[1] (David Spangler, *Reflections on the Christ*, p. 45)
http://searchlight.iwarp.com/articles/na_plan.html#initiation or death
[2] Liberty To The Captives
It Appears Christians Will Not Have the Mark of the Beast?
http://www.libertytothecaptives.net/tim_lahaye_false_teaching_mark_of_beast.html
[3] Liberty To The Captives
Tim LaHaye's False Teachings About the Mark of the Beast in His Book, Are We Living in the End Times?
http://www.libertytothecaptives.net/tim_lahaye_are_we_living_in_the_end_times.html
[4] http://www.freerepublic.com/forum/a360d496e0c97.htm)

Chapter 11 – The Antichrist Foundation Of The *Left Behind* Series

[1] David Wilkerson's Times Square Pulpit Series (World Challenge Pubs, Linsdale Tex), Apr. 15, 2002

Chapter 12 – Merging With The Kingdom Of Antichrist

[1] Propaganda Techniques: Rationalization
http://www.freerepublic.com/forum/a360d496e0c97.htm
[2] Luciferic Initiation Energy Activation Rebirth
http://www.cephasministry.com/new_age_initiation.html

Chapter 13 – New Age Markings On *Left Behind*

[1] http://www3.bc.sympatico.ca/thegoodnews/newage.htm
[2] Liberty To The Captives
Left Behind's New Age Gospel
http://www.libertytothecaptives.net/new_age_left_behind_gospel.html
[3] Make a Choice (The Plan archives)
http://web.archive.org/web/20010803220155/www.leftbehind.com/make_choice.html
[4] Prayer Circles: Small Groups
http://www.piney.com/ChCircles.html
[5] Transcendental Meditation: Hinduism in a Scientist's Smock
http://www.mcbryan.co.uk/tm-info/tmpmeans.htm
[6] Gail Riplinger, *New Age Bible Versions* (AV Publications, Va., 1993), p. 78

[7] The Reappearance of the Christ
    http://www.lucistrust.org/arcane/roc.shtml
[8] The Great Invocation (Long Version)
    http://web.singnet.com.sg/~sweeb/invocation.html
[9] Ibid.
[10] William Evans, *The Great Doctrines of the Bible* (Moody Press, Chicago, 1912)

This page provided for your thoughts and prayers while reading
GOD'S WRATH ON *LEFT BEHIND*

To purchase additional copies of
GOD'S WRATH ON *LEFT BEHIND*
Visit our website at
http://www.libertytothecaptives.net

or

Contact us by mail at
Liberty To The Captives Publications
224 Reservoir Street
North Attleborough, MA 02760